THE BAROQUE LANDSCAPE

In cooperation with the Fachhochschule München / University of Applied Sciences, Munich

The Baroque Landscape

André Le Nôtre & Vaux le Vicomte

Michael Brix

Translated by Steven Lindberg

RIZZOLI
NEW YORK

Nicolas Fouquet, the creator of Vaux le Vicomte, is the hero of this domain. Thus I try to revive the spirit of his inspiration, the traces of his epoch, the decorations he chose for his residence and his garden, and the voices of his friends in these beautiful, evocative places. But do we, living in the twenty-first century, have the capacity to separate ourselves from three centuries of judgments and new contributions and see with the eyes of the seventeenth century?

Michael Brix is someone who sees more clearly than others; his study casts a rare, original, and passionate light on the gardens of Vaux le Vicomte; he too has been attracted by the adventure of this model garden that Louis XIV strove to surpass at Versailles, for on August 17, 1661, the most beautiful residence in France was indeed Vaux le Vicomte.

Today the rivalry belongs to a historic past, and Vaux le Vicomte continues to shine. The grammar of the classical French garden, mapped out here by André Le Nôtre, has been propagated in variants throughout Europe; this place has always been dominated by the equilibrium, the harmony, and the beauty whose inspirations Michael Brix reveals to us.

Comte Patrice de Vogüé
Château de Vaux le Vicomte

The university that I direct cultivates partnerships with several French institutions, including the EPF École d'Ingénieurs in Sceaux. This place is profoundly marked by one of André Le Nôtre's masterpieces. The grand and stunning perspectives of the park in Sceaux have always impressed me, but the message that the artist who created this garden wanted to communicate was always obscure to me. The work of my colleague Michael Brix has opened up new horizons of understanding for me. Now I too know that everything begins at Vaux le Vicomte. From here the paths lead to many of Europe's former noble residences, to Munich as well, where the *style Le Nôtre* is present at the Schloss Nymphenburg.

Our university has set itself the goal of cultivating its international relationships even more vigorously than before. André Le Nôtre may be considered an important ambassador of a culture that crossed borders — that is, a European one. That is why we lent our support to this project on French gardens. We were also interested in its interdisciplinary aspects: the connections between the fields of technology, mathematics, and philosophy.

For our university, which is focused on the disciplines of technology and the economy, the support of this kind of cultural project certainly represents an adventure. Our enthusiasm, however, has not wavered, and we are delighted that we supported this effort.

The realization of this project would not have been possible without the expert assistance that Comte Patrice de Vogüé, the owner of the château of Vaux le Vicomte, has generously offered over the years.

Prof. Dr. Marion Schick
President, Fachhochschule München / University of Applied Sciences, Munich

»The buildings, the furniture, the silver, and the other decorations were only available to the financiers and tax farmers, for which they gave out prodigious sums, while His Majesty's buildings were often behind the times for lack of money; indeed, the royal houses were not furnished at all, and there was not even a pair of silver andirons for the king's chamber.«

Jean-Baptiste Colbert (1619–1683)

»1875 / Testimony to the French genius, / this beautiful place / commissioned by Fouquet / sung by La Fontaine / long neglected / and on which nature had reclaimed its rights / has been restored to their classical splendor / by the love and care of two generations.« These lines, engraved on a commemorative plaque found at the edge of Vaux le Vicomte's garden, at the Parterre de la Couronne, set the tone that has always reigned here: it is the culture of the era that the French proudly call the Grand Siècle. Vaux le Vicomte is a *Gesamtkunstwerk* of truly majestic ambitions; its author is not King Louis XIV, however, but one of his subjects: his superintendent of finance, Nicolas Fouquet.

Fouquet is one of the most famous personalities in French history. The trial he faced, which ended with a ruthless executive judgment from the king, was one of the most spectacular trials of the seventeenth century, and it occupies writers and historians even today. »Fouquet is the liveliest of men, the most natural, the most tolerant, the most brilliant, the most gifted in the art of living, the most French.«[1] This picture of the superintendent, by the writer Paul Morand, accords with the portrait that the engraver Robert Nanteuil made in 1661 — the year in which Fouquet gave his famous fête at Vaux le Vicomte and in which he was arrested. On this portrait the superintendent presents himself in simple clothing, with gleaming eyes and a smile; he does not retreat behind the impenetrable mask that other political dignitaries of the age wore, like Armand-Jean du Plessis de Richelieu, Jules Mazarin, or Jean-Baptiste Colbert.

PREVIOUS PAGE:
Fame, sculpture in the garden of the Tuileries, Paris, by Antoine Coysevox, 1702 (copy)

LEFT:
Nicolas Fouquet, engraving by Robert Nanteuil, 1661 (detail)

OPPOSITE:
The main portal of the château at Vaux

ABOVE:
The garden facade of the château
at Vaux

OPPOSITE:
Louis XIV, marble bust by
Gianlorenzo Bernini, 1665

Nicolas Fouquet had a brilliant political career. In 1650 he purchased the office of attorney general in the Parliament of Paris and thereby became one of the king's representatives at the supreme court. During the Fronde — the revolt by members of parliament and the aristocracy against the king from 1648 to 1653 — he remained loyal to the ruling house, and by doing so he played a decisive role in restoring its authority and thus clearing a path for the young Louis XIV. In 1653 the prime minister, Cardinal Mazarin, named Fouquet superintendent of finance. He shared this office with Abel Servien, who was more than twenty years older. His task was primarily to raise money, while Servien was responsible for distributing it. The task was nearly impossible, because the administration of finances was in ruins and characterized by continual improvisation. When Servien died in February 1659 Fouquet remained as the sole holder of the office. He hoped for even more — namely, being named Cardinal Mazarin's successor.

The château, the garden, and the park of Vaux le Vicomte were intended as external signs of Fouquet's rise, and as anticipation of the rewards that the superintendent believed he was entitled to expect for demonstrating his fidelity and loyalty to the king. He took things too far, however. At the time, none of the king's residences could compare to the modernity and elegance of Vaux le Vicomte — Versailles was still a modest hunting château surrounded by swamps. The contrast revealed all too clearly the fragility of the king's power at the beginning of Louis XIV's reign.

ABOVE:
Project by Charles Le Brun for the
painting in the cupola of the Grand
Salon in the château at Vaux,
engraving by Gérard Audran, 1681
(Detail)

RIGHT:
The Grand Salon in the château at Vaux

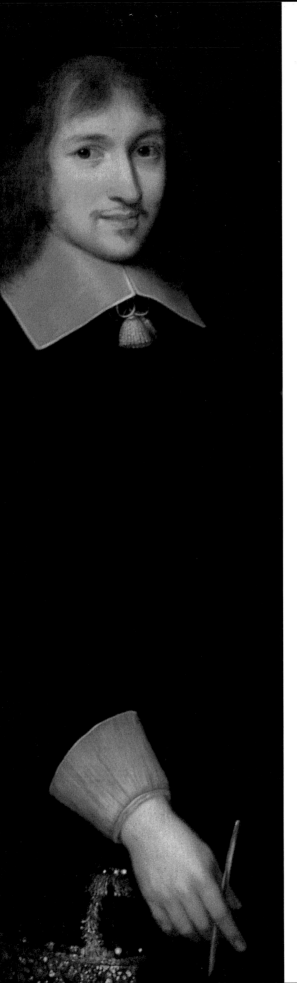

Nicolas Fouquet had acquired the domain Vaux le Vicomte in 1641. It consisted of a modest water château, along with a village and several rustic buildings. Everything that stood in the way of the total work of art that was the new landlord's dream has disappeared without a trace; today, it is no longer even possible to specify precisely where the old château stood. Thierry Mariage commented on this: »This notion of a tabula rasa initiates a new mode of thinking that will become the way of centralized power.«[2] Fouquet intended to make Vaux le Vicomte his ceremonial residence: »Vaux […] is the place I considered my principal residence […] and where I wanted to leave some mark of the estate I had achieved.«[3] With the fine sense of a patron of the arts, Fouquet appointed three important artists for the remodeling of his property: the architect Louis Le Vau, the painter Charles Le Brun, and the gardener André Le Nôtre, who would collaborate closely in realizing his *Gesamtkunstwerk*.

LEFT:
Nicolas Fouquet, painting by an
anonymous master, circa 1660
(detail)

OPPOSITE:
Portico of the eastern part of the
Communs (outbuildings) of the
château at Vaux

General map of the domain of Vaux from 1754 (above)
and a modern survey photograph (opposite)

»And because it is appropriate to determine the time when he [Fouquet]
spent these great sums, it should be noted first that he acquired Vaux when
he was still master of petitions / That a little while later he made some payments
for the construction of a lower court, a parterre, a grove of hornbeams, a kitchen
garden, and an orchard; and that all of this was enclosed by walls and consisted of
a good forty or fifty acres / But also that immediately on entering office as
superintendent he conceived a grander plan — in order to carry it out,
the course of the water was regulated during the years 1653 and 1654 [. . .].«

Archives of Olivier Lefèvre d'Ormesson, after 1661

THE ORIGINAL GARDEN AND
ITS REDESIGN IN MORE ELABORATE STYLE

Immediately on taking office as superintendent of finance in 1653 Nicolas Fouquet ordered a new, more ambitious plan — »un plus grand dessein« — for the completion of the garden at Vaux. The evidence of this is a valuable document that is found in the Archives nationales in Paris. It was drawn up by Olivier Lefèvre d'Ormesson during the trial against Fouquet. This as yet unpublished source, to which the historian Jean-Christian Petitfils had called attention, is a detailed report on the works that were carried out at Vaux le Vicomte between 1653 and 1661. D'Ormesson gives precise details of the state in which the garden was found in 1653 and to what extent it had been redesigned thereafter. Combining an assessment of the report with a stylistic analysis of the garden makes it clear beyond all doubt that the garden was designed by André Le Nôtre.

The question of when Le Nôtre began work at Vaux is passionately debated in the literature; the proposals range from 1653 and 1656.[4] Multiple sources show, however, that Le Nôtre arrived at Vaux in 1652 or 1653. Jean-Marie Pérouse de Montclos dates the beginning of his activity to »c. 1653,« and he bases this on a brief biography written by Claude Desgots, Le Nôtre's nephew, and published by Père Desmolets in his *Continuation des mémoires de littérature et d'histoire.*[5] According to Desgots, Le Nôtre, who was born on March 12, 1613, was »nearly forty years old« when Fouquet commissioned him: that would mean Le Nôtre arrived at Vaux in 1653 at the latest and perhaps as early as 1652. This is confirmed by Dezallier d'Argenville, who states precisely in his book *Voyage pittoresque des environs de Paris* (1762 ed.) that Le Nôtre was thirty-nine when he was called to Vaux.[6]

PREVIOUS PAGE:
Summer, sculpture in the garden at Vaux, eighteenth century

ABOVE:
André Le Nôtre, marble bust by Antoine Coysevox (1708) in the church of Saint-Roch, Paris

OPPOSITE:
View over the forecourt of the château at Vaux toward the garden

The realization of the new, expanded plan that Fouquet desired called for extensive changes to parts of the garden that were already finished. D'Ormesson's report states: »that immediately on entering office as superintendent he conceived a still grander plan — in order to carry it out, the course of the water was regulated during the years 1653 and 1654; it was made to pass through a bed [. . .] to flow into the canal and extend the parterre; they undertook a search for the waters coming from the springs near Melun to supply the fountains; they began to collect soil to unify the flower parterres; and the extension of the grand parterre with the small canals, the parterre and the flower garden, the fountains, the wall around the park, and the large terraced allée near Moisenay were carried out in 1655« (156 MI 18, fol. 79 recto–79 verso).

As is evident from this report, the first measure undertaken was the subterranean canalization of a watercourse, the stream from Jumeaux that crossed the meadow bordering the garden to the east. This stream was directed into the Anqueil, a small river that was not dammed to form a canal until 1655. After the stream had been canalized, it became possible to construct in 1655 those parts of the park that border on the village of Moisenay and the properties that belonged to it. One of these measures was the construction of a »grande allée en terrasse« (large terraced allée). The location line of the allée had to be artificially leveled out in the rough terrain, which fell off sharply toward the Anqueil; that is why on the *Parc de Villars* plan it is described as a »grande terrasse.« The allée leads to the place at the edge of the garden where the Confessionnal would later be constructed.

ABOVE:
View from the eastern end of the Grand Canal at Vaux toward the Anqueil River

OPPOSITE:
Plan of the garden at Vaux, Moisenay parish and the village of Maincy (*Parc de Pra[s]lin* plan), circa 1780

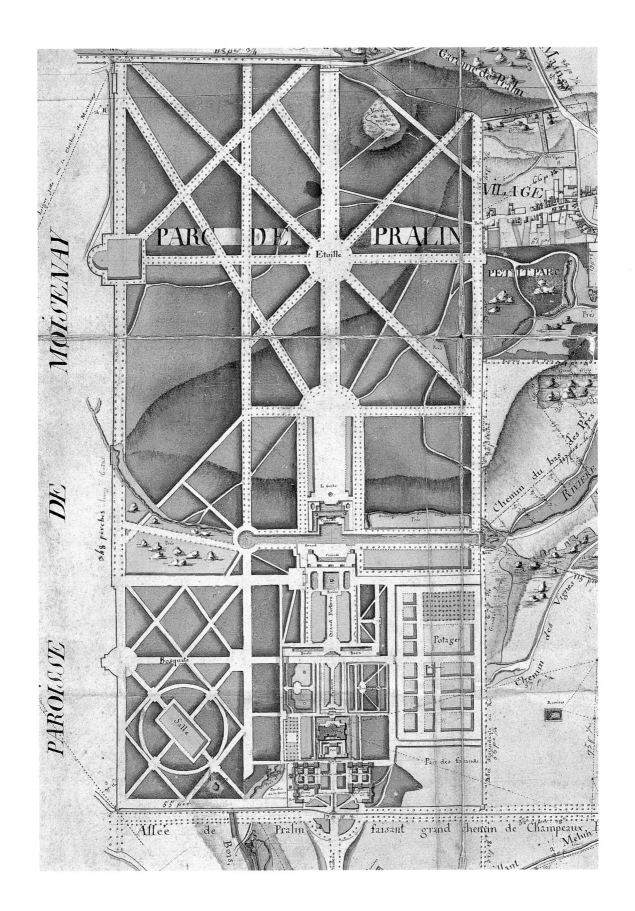

From d'Ormesson's description it is clear which parterres already existed when Le Nôtre began his work in the garden — namely, the three parterres that stretched out before the château: in the middle the large parterre (that is, the embroidery parterre); a parterre in the east, namely, the present Parterre de la Couronne; and finally the flower parterre in the west. Beginning in 1653 Le Nôtre redesigned these parterres, applying his distinctive style to them.

The most important measure undertaken was no doubt the redesign of the large parterre, which Le Nôtre extended considerably toward the south, giving it a form that was very unusual for the age. Until that time it was common to design such a parterre as a self-contained unity: a square that was subdivided into four beds with a fountain or pool at the center. Le Nôtre, by contrast, designed an elongated embroidery parterre that is divided into just two parts, with a symmetrical axis that is powerfully emphasized. This marks the start of the central axis that dominates the whole garden to the horizon. This axis is also emphasized by the group of three round pools: two small pools to the side at the beginning of the parterre, which have vanished today, and in the central axis another, considerably larger, pool at the end of the parterre. This arrangement reinforces the impression that the parterre moves in one direction — namely, into the depth of the garden.

View from the cupola of the château at Vaux over the embroidery parterre

This composition of the embroidery parterre is one of the characteristic innovations that Le Nôtre introduced to the art of the garden. Very similar designs are found in his later works — for example, in his plans for Saint-Germain-en-Laye, Clagny, and especially Versailles, where there was originally — in the 1660s —such an embroidery parterre by Le Nôtre, though it was transformed into a water parterre by Charles Le Brun in 1671 and later modified again.

In his report d'Ormesson uses a clear terminology to identify the individual elements of the garden. When he speaks of the »parterre,« as opposed to the »grand parterre,« he means the one that would later be called the Parterre de la Couronne. Its composition points clearly to Le Nôtre's hand; according to Gerold Weber, it can be »characterized as the very leitmotif of Le Nôtre's parterre design.«[7] The dominant figure is a large oval, to which the swaying lines of the two lawn beds conform. Likewise, the trees and hedges are planted to form a spacious exedra. Once again there are three pools, one of the artist's favorite motifs: two small ones and a large one. In contrast to the embroidery parterre, whose axis leads into the depths of the garden — that is, to the south — the lateral parterre defines a transverse axis that draws the viewer's eye to the east. Here Le Nôtre created a structure of parts that are opposed to one another and yet complementary. This style of composing a garden, which may be characterized as contrapuntal, was unprecedented in 1655; Le Nôtre would also come to use it later in several of his large creations, such as the gardens of Meudon and Sceaux.

When d'Ormesson reports on enlarging the large parterre and extending the Parterre de la Couronne, he provides a clue to understanding a strange irregularity that the garden once had, which can be seen most clearly from the *Parc de Villars* plan (see Documentation, p. 172). Here the Parterre de la Couronne is depicted with the southern lawn bed significantly broader than the northern one, even though the parterre has a clear symmetrical axis. The situation is similar with the flower parterre. These conspicuous irregularities now have a simple explanation: After Le Nôtre extended the embroidery parterre, he pragmatically adjusted the two lateral parterres accordingly, which destroyed their symmetry. As part of the restoration carried out around 1900 these inconsistencies were eliminated, but at the cost of producing another (see Documentation, p. 174).

Aerial photograph of the château
and garden at Vaux (south to north)

In 1656 work began on extending the garden to the south. From a purchase agreement it is clear that Nicolas Fouquet acquired »the pond of Vaux [. . .] and the adjoining properties.«[8] This pond was found in the central part of what would become the Grand Canal. According to d'Ormesson's report, construction of the château began in 1656. The architect Daniel Gittard is mentioned in this context, along with Bénigne Courtois, the intendant of Vaux, and it indicates that both were also involved in the further development of the garden in »that the first cascade, the water square and the rivulets, the leveled meadow, the walls, and the steps that support the terrace were also made by this same Gittard and by Courtois in 1656 und 1657« (156 MI 18, fol. 79 verso).

Hence the »first cascade,« that is, the Grille d'eau, was constructed at the eastern end of the transverse axis that separates the first zone of the parterre from the adjacent one; the other tasks that d'Ormesson lists pertain to

the second zone of the garden. The former meadow, which descended to the vale of the Anqueil River, was graded and transformed into an esplanade, so that the lawn parterre could be laid out; the terrace was provided with a retaining wall to the west. In addition, according to the report, they also constructed a »water square,« that is, the large square pool, and the »rivulets,« that is, the small canals that were designed to shoot up jets of water and form the Allée d'eau, which no longer exists today.

The lawn parterre of the garden at Vaux

The second zone of the garden — even more than the first — reveals several characteristic features that make it clear Vaux le Vicomte represents a milestone in the history of the art of gardening. In relation to the parterres and the pools of the garden's first zone, the corresponding areas of the second zone are considerably larger in scale. Le Nôtre used the method of *perspective ralentie*, decelerated perspective, with a rigor that no artist before him had shown (on *perspective ralentie*, see p. 88).

The design of lawn beds without any ornamentation at all is so unusual that there is hardly anything comparable even in Le Nôtre's later works. At Versailles, for example, he would create lawn parterres whose ornamental motifs are inscribed like palmettes and arabesques; likewise the great parterre of the Orangerie, which was reconstructed in 2001.

Finally, it is worth noting that the element should dominate in a lawn parterre: canals and the watery surfaces of pools, as well as the famous Allée d'eau, with its shooting jets of water, which once underscored the central axis but is now replaced by rows of marble bowls. The square pool is of truly gigantic dimensions, more than two hundred feet in each direction. The surfaces of water are Le Nôtre's primary means for achieving the effects of *perspective ralentie*.

LEFT:
Survey photograph of the garden at Vaux

OPPOSITE:
The parterre of the Orangerie at Versailles

D'Ormesson's report does not just offer precise information about the genesis of the garden from 1653 on; it also contains a summary description of what had been done up to that point. This description exposes as mere legends all the conjectures about a great garden that supposedly existed before Le Nôtre's arrival at Vaux. Certainly there were already parterres in front of the château, but Le Nôtre altered them so fundamentally that no traces of his predecessors' work remain.

The second zone of the garden, as d'Ormesson's indications clearly confirm, was created ex nihilo from 1656 on; here Le Nôtre could realize his innovative ideas without any precedents. It remains a question, however, what should be attributed to the architect Daniel Gittard. D'Ormesson reports that the plans in the second part of the garden were »made« by Gittard, and this documentary evidence recently led the historian Petitfils to draw a momentous but nonetheless mistaken conclusion: »Le Nôtre's role in the conception of what is generally accepted as the first French garden ultimately remains unclear. It is certain that he intervened only after the framework had been staked out by Gittard; thus he should not be seen as the garden's creator but as its brilliant organizer.«[9]

Although d'Ormesson mentions Le Nôtre's name in his report just once, stylistic analysis nonetheless demonstrates that the plan should without reservation be viewed as his work and that Daniel Gittard, whom d'Ormesson also calls the »entrepreneur,« was responsible only for directing the construction. It is known that Gittard later — in the 1670s and 1680s — collaborated with Le Nôtre at Chantilly, but there too, as Bertrand Jestaz demonstrated recently, his role was primarily limited to directing the work in accordance with plans by Le Nôtre and Jules Hardouin-Mansart.[10]

The garden at Vaux, seen from the château's cupola

»Bernini wanted to meet Le Nôtre. The latter, when paying him a visit, was pleasantly surprised to find on the great man's desk the collection of prints depicting some of his works. Bernini told him he did not know who the author was, but that they partook of a rare genius.«

Père Desmolets, 1726

»The excellence of his works was his response to the grandeur and magnificence of Louis le Grand, who lavished him with honors and gifts. France is not the only one to have profited from his rare talents; all the princes of Europe wanted to have his designs and those of his students. He had no rival who might have equaled him.«

Inscription on Le Nôtres memorial epitaph in the church of Saint-Roch, Paris, after 1700

In *Voyage pittoresque des environs de Paris* Dezallier d'Argenville says of Versailles: »The gardens were planted by Le Nôtre, this felicitous genius whom one might call the creator of the art of the garden.«[11] The inscription chiseled on Le Nôtre's epitaph in the church of Saint-Roch, Paris, is similar: »The power and scope of his genius made him so unique in the art of the garden that he may be regarded as having invented its chief forms of beauty and as having brought the others to their ultimate perfection.«[12] These eulogies can only be understood if their emphasis is noted: Le Nôtre raised garden design to the rank of a high art.

The stylistic features of the parterres at Vaux le Vicomte demonstrate the important innovations that Le Nôtre bequeathed the gardener's repertoire. But what about those »other« forms of beauty, that is, the principles of designing gardens that Le Nôtre inherited from his predecessors and brought »to their ultimate perfection«? In order to clarify this question it may be useful to look at the two gardens that are considered to be Vaux le Vicomte's most important predecessors.

PREVIOUS PAGE:
Statue of André Le Nôtre (late nineteenth century) in the garden at Chantilly

LEFT:
André Le Nôtre, painting by Carlo Maratta, 1678 (detail)

OPPOSITE:
The Grand Degré (large stairway) in the garden at Versailles

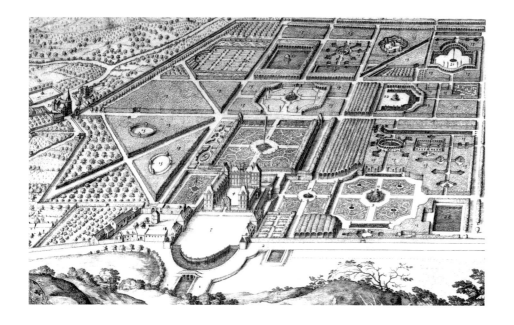

There are few surviving illustrations or descriptions of the gardens dating from the first half of the seventeenth century. In terms of size Liancourt (1630s) is the only one of these gardens that could be compared to Vaux le Vicomte. There is a large embroidery parterre in front of the château; it is divided into four parts with a pool at the center. This is followed by a terrace on a lower level, described as a »place,« which is also divided into four parts and has a pool. The terrace is designed as a closed space, fenced in by rows of pruned trees. The flower parterre, in an isolated area east of the château, is rather modest. Two more parterres of substantial size extend to the west of the château: an embroidery parterre and a lawn parterre, equipped with fountains and cascades.

Liancourt, one of the most beautiful seventeenth-century residences in Île-de-France, »already prefigures Vaux le Vicomte in many respects,« as Gisèle Caumont rightly notes.[13] The differences that Gerold Weber persuasively describes, are equally manifest.[14] In his view the parterres are lined up additively; allées separate the various spaces of the garden, which are treated as completely autonomous units. Le Nôtre, by contrast, connects the parts of the garden; he treats them as dynamic elements that contribute to a unified and clearly arranged space.

ABOVE:
Château and garden at Liancourt (1630s),
engraving by Henri Mauperché

OPPOSITE:
Aerial photograph of the château and garden
at Vaux (north to south)

Of the architectural ensembles that point prototypically to Vaux, the château and garden of Richelieu (1630s) are especially important. Particularly majestic in its effect is the large axis that connects the château to the town and continues beyond the garden. In front of the château the axis expands to form a round plaza, from which two additional allées radiate diagonally outward. This *patte d'oie* (goose foot) became a leitmotif in Le Nôtre's landscapes at Vaux le Vicomte, Versailles, and Chantilly. The garden of Richelieu is of only moderate size. A square parterre, surrounded by moats and decorated with flowers, is followed by the embroidery parterre. The latter is a masterpiece of the genre. It has the concise form of a stilted arch, and in this figure is inscribed a perfect circle that is divided into four parts. Both parterres are proportioned according to *perspective ralentie*: a rare example of the use of this method before Le Nôtre.

In the first half of the seventeenth century the theory of the art of gardening reached a high level. Le Nôtre was, of course, familiar with the treatises of Claude I Mollet, Jacques Boyceau, André Mollet, and others, and they provided him with important ideas. Certainly Le Nôtre was able to benefit from the legacy of the generation of gardeners who had already formulated several essential principles of the French garden. However, the frequently expressed opinion that he merely refined these principles and incorporated them into a logical system does not do justice to his work. He truly revolutionized the art of the garden — in harmony with the stylistic tendencies of European baroque art.

ABOVE:
The large semicircular parterre at
Richelieu (1630s), engraving by Perelle

OPPOSITE:
General plan of the château at Richelieu
(1630s), engraving by Jean Marot

It was Nicolas Fouquet who gave Le Nôtre, then nearly forty, the opportunity to realize his ideas of a new art of gardening, not just at Vaux le Vicomte, where the superintendent wanted to receive his guests officially, but probably also at Saint-Mandé, his private residence near the château of Vincennes, which he purchased in 1654. That same year Fouquet entrusted the architect Louis Le Vau with redesigning the buildings. In contrast to the house, which was rather modest, the garden was imposing, as is evident from a large plan dating from 1663,[15] even though its dimensions — roughly 360 feet long — could not be compared with those of Vaux le Vicomte. Nevertheless, both gardens share a number of characteristic features that are typical of Le Nôtre's style.

The parterres, terraces, and paths at Saint-Mandé were, like those at Vaux, larger as one moved further from the entrance. Its embroidery parterre, also like that at Vaux, was not divided into four parts; instead, it had a distinct mirror axis, which was reinforced by the motif of mirrored volutes. It is also striking that the large, round pool is placed neither in the center of the embroidery parterre nor in the middle of the adjacent terrace but between them, which connects these two zones of the garden and forms an autonomous accent in the central axis. The ornaments of the two lawn parterres are very similar to those Le Nôtre would use several years later, from 1663 on, in the garden of the Tuileries. One very striking element of the plan for Saint-Mandé is the large, exquisitely ornamented kitchen garden, which is without parallel among the works that are definitely by Le Nôtre. Nevertheless, the other correspondences justify the assumption that it was Le Nôtre whom Nicolas Fouquet commissioned to design this other garden, which was contemporaneous with Vaux le Vicomte.

Vaux le Vicomte is, as Dezallier d'Argenville has remarked, »Le Nôtre's first extensive work,«[16] and at the same time it represents, as Kenneth Woodbridge has pronounced, »the ultimate achievement of French classical garden design.«[17] Walking through the garden, from the grille at the entrance to the statue of Hercules that adds the final accent at the far end of the park, one experiences with each step how artfully Le Nôtre manipulated the landscape in order to surprise the visitor with a continuous alternation of hiding and revealing.

ABOVE:
Plan of the garden at Saint-Mandé, drawing with watercolor, dated 1663; the kitchen garden is to the right of the plan

OPPOSITE:
Portico of the western part of the Communs of the château at Vaux

»When one is in this forecourt, one sees before one the facade of the palace,

which is built on a mountain formed by architecture, it must be said,

because the flight of stairs, which takes up the full width of the second courtyard,

has four podiums and is more than twenty steps high. This lends the building

great majesty. [. . .] Indeed, [. . .] there is nothing more grand or

magnificent than to see [. . .] this second courtyard [. . .] and its grand

and magnificent flight of stairs that traverses the entire courtyard,

this flight of stairs, I tell you, which rises so majestically, and from which

one looks in the center of the palace a grand vestibule with three magnificent

arcades, supported by six columns, through which the eye can see across

the entire depth of the palace, through three more arcades, opposite

the first three, and then three more again opposite these; so that the sky,

seen through these various openings, is all the more agreeable.«

Madeleine de Scudéry, 1661

The iron gates, terms, and portals that confine the forecourt of the château form a remarkable ensemble (see ill. on p. 41). The portals, off to the sides, have no practical function. It is impossible to enter the forecourt of the château through them, since the rather high stone thresholds provide obstacles, and the wrought-iron gates do not move. It is the grille in the middle, much less monumental than the portals, through which one enters the court. The visitor to Vaux le Vicomte is thus already, here at the entrance, being readied for a play of surprises and illusory appearances.

The eight sandstone pillars that support busts of divinities, fauns, and allegories of the seasons are the work of the sculptors Thibault Poissant and Mathieu Lespagnandel. These terms are Janus-faced, facing both the château and the pitch beyond the forecourt, like guards who seem to have come from an ancient world of myth. Several of the figures seem cyclopean, which is reinforced by their unfinished state. The architect Rudolf Pfnor noted the following findings in 1888: »Of the sixteen heads [. . .] only three or four are fully complete; the others are merely more or less roughhewn.«[18] Several of them were reworked during the restoration campaign in the late nineteenth and early twentieth centuries, and today, according to Patricia Brattig's research, only a few busts can be identified with certainty: Hercules, Apollo, Minerva, Flora, Ceres, and two fauns.[19] These terms have their pendant in the eight atlantes of the grotto that provide the last architectural accent in the furthest part of the garden. This establishes a subtle connection between the entrance and the garden.

Already in antiquity, terms were destined to be placed outdoors, and since the early sixteenth century, the garden was the preferred location for them — beautiful examples include the nymphaeum of the Villa Giulia in Rome, the garden of the Palazzina Farnese in Caprarola, and the Pegasus Fountain of the Villa Lante in Bagnaia. In the garden of Vaux le Vicomte in Le Nôtre's day, terms were almost omnipresent from the first parterres to the lawn amphitheater above the grotto. Even in the château they were assigned an important role: a ring of stucco terms under the vault of the Grand Salon identifies it as a kind of garden hall. Most of the terms in the garden have been relocated today. Twelve of them, formerly in the lawn parterre, were executed according to designs by Nicolas Poussin; this famous cycle is now in the garden at Versailles (see Documentation, pp. 165–66).

ABOVE:
The entrance grille of the château at Vaux,
with the Janus-faced terms

OPPOSITE:
The nymphaeum of the Villa Giulia, Rome

51

The ensemble of terms, iron grilles, and the double-winged gate with its rich wrought-iron ornaments is subtly matched to the château, as Franklin Hamilton Hazlehurst has demonstrated in detail:[20] they do not close off the forecourt but form a transparent fence. It poses no obstacle to the large central axis that passes through it, which begins well in front of the château, penetrates its center (the vestibule and the Grand Salon), and continues like a line of force to the end of the garden. This axis, which dominates everything, giving the whole layout of Vaux a strong unity, is probably the product of a collaboration between the architect, Louis Le Vau, and the artist of the garden, Le Nôtre.

Certainly there are several earlier examples in France of similar dispositions, in which the château was tied into a large axis that began in the approach and continued in the garden — Richelieu and Maisons are great examples of this. But in Vaux le Vicomte the axis is emphasized even more by the specific design of the vestibule and the Grand Salon: the salon originally opened onto the garden through arcades that had grilles, not French doors as they do today; these arcades corresponded to those that connected the salon to the vestibule. When the entrance doors were open on the courtyard side, one could see through the whole building to the end of the garden.

Entrance grille and château at Vaux

By designing the central section of the château such that it was open to the central axis, Louis Le Vau was referring directly to the garden, and he certainly did this, as we have mentioned, in close consultation with André Le Nôtre. Other works by this architect show a similar design, particularly the great wall in the southern courtyard of the château at Vincennes, which was built around the same time as Vaux le Vicomte. At Vincennes the arcades, which penetrate the wall on both sides of the portal, offer impressive views into the park.

The transparence of the château in its central section already attracted the attention of Le Nôtre's contemporaries: with remarkable accuracy Madeleine de Scudéry described the wonderful effect of the arcades of the vestibule and the salon, which are precisely coordinated to each other: »the sky, seen through these various openings, is all the more agreeable.«[21] Madeleine de Scudéry's observations are confirmed by contemporary engravings: in the front view of the château by Israël Silvestre one sees through the building into the garden (see Documentation, p. 169), and in the engraving by Adam Perelle, which presents an elevated perspective of the château, the arcades are all open.

Wall in the southern courtyard of the château at Vincennes

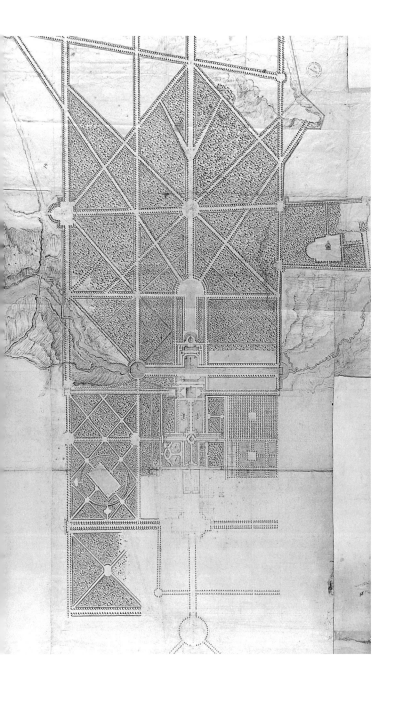

The old plans of Vaux le Vicomte demonstrate particularly impressively the importance that Le Nôtre and Le Vau attributed to the central axis, which not only ran through the garden from beginning to end but originally extended far beyond. As the plan in the Institut de France shows, the allée in front of the château was originally supposed to lead into a roundabout, and from there two additional allées were to branch off diagonally. At the very end of the garden, behind the statue of Hercules, this pattern was to be repeated: here a half-moon, a large semicircular plaza, was planned; there in the adjacent park followed a star-shaped plaza; and finally a *patte d'oie*, with three allées radiating outward. On the plan in the Institut the half-moon that concludes the garden and the roundabout in front of the château had the same diameter; on the plan by Israël Silvestre the château marks exactly the midpoint between these two plazas.

Here at Vaux le Vicomte we encounter the first of the extended and hierarchically structured spaces that are so typical of Le Nôtre, of which Versailles is the most impressive example. Thierry Mariage has rightly compared this manner of shaping space with »modern methods of urbanization and contemporary planning.«[22]

When visitors look out over the garden from the château, they see before them an enormous open esplanade that is demarcated by a wall designed like a grotto. Beyond this wall the terrain rises and is crowned by a colossal statue of Hercules, more than half a mile from the château (see ill. on pp. 34–35).

As far as the eye can see, the open space of the garden is surrounded by forest. It is difficult to imagine that the terrain was originally completely bare; Fouquet had it reforested, which decisively altered the topography. Contemporary drawings and engravings reveal that the trees were planted in stages, beginning next to the first parterre zone and ending on the hills beyond the canal. The forest by no means isolates the garden but rather creates a frame of immeasurable depth, which gives it the feel of a spacious clearing.

View from the elevated section of the garden toward the château at Vaux

»Indeed, it is impossible to imagine that Valterre [Vaux le Vicomte] could be
one of those places that Nature has made attractive almost entirely on her own;
on the contrary, one can say without exaggeration that Cléonime [Fouquet]
transformed it entirely, and that there is not one place where he did not
add some new charm. He divided a river into a thousand fountains; he reunited
the thousand fountains into torrents; and he arranged all that he did at Valterre
so judiciously that one cannot adequately praise the judgment of the man
who understood how to unite the beauties of Art and those of Nature.«

Madeleine de Scudéry, 1661

»Behind the large square pool one descends further, and one sees
something completely surprising. Indeed, the imagination cannot conceive
anything so grand, so agreeable, so magnificent; Nature, as omnipotent as she is,
cannot produce anything so beautiful; and art, which often prides itself
on imitating her, of surpassing her sometimes, and embellishing her always,
could never create anything this marvelous. Thus one can say that what
one sees here is a masterpiece of Art and Nature joined together.«

Madeleine de Scudéry, 1661

NATURE CIVILIZED

The garden is dominated by the art of planar composition. There are no monumental fountains or groups of towering sculpture that would hold one's gaze above the level parterres. Only the cones and pyramids of yews, which reach considerable heights today, provide any vertical accents, but they only obtained these voluminous forms during the restoration of the late nineteenth and early twentieth centuries. Hence the impression of extended planes was originally even more emphatic, and this is one of the most striking features of all the large gardens Le Nôtre designed; his most radical creations in this respect were the extended water parterres of Chantilly (see ill. on p. 75).

Although the garden of Vaux le Vicomte has very imposing structures like the grotto and the cascade, they do not tower over the terrain but are, rather, so perfectly integrated into it that they present no barriers to the overall perspective of the garden.

PREVIOUS PAGE AND ABOVE:
Views of the lawn parterre
in the garden at Vaux

The water parterre in the garden at Versailles

Le Nôtre's distinct preference for unobstructed spaces astonished his contemporaries. For example, the duc de Saint-Simon polemically described the water parterre at Versailles as »a giant plane like a desert,«[23] and the *Mercure galant* wrote in September 1700, on the occasion of Le Nôtre's death: »He never permitted as much covering in the gardens he executed as some might wish, but he could not bear restricted views and did not feel that beautiful gardens should at all resemble forests.«[24]

The viewer's gaze will be drawn first to the *broderies*, which recall embroidery or Oriental carpets. They are not one of Le Nôtre's inventions, as it was common in France even before his time to decorate the area immediately in front of a château in this way. The introduction of embroideries in France is discussed in Claude I Mollet's treatise *Théâtre des plans et jardinages*, written around 1610 but published posthumously in 1652. Mollet observes that the architect Étienne du Pérac taught him in the 1580s that parterres should no longer be assembled additively from small square beds but should fit together as elements of a comprehensive ornamental unity. Mollet writes further that he first used boxwood at Saint-Germain-en-Laye in 1595 to make the main ornamental lines of the design in the beds.[25] Boxwood has been common ever since the contours of embroideries — »for their construction,« as André Mollet expressed it in his treatise *Le jardin de plaisir* of 1651.[26] This treatise reveals that around 1650 — that is, at the start of Le Nôtre's era — it was still quite common to fill the ornaments created by boxwood with small patches of lawn and flowers or low-growing plants, and that sand of various colors was used to fill the remaining interstices.[27]

Many of the plates that illustrate the treatises of Jacques Boyceau (1638) and André Mollet (1651) are devoted to embroidery parterres. Embroideries were then considered the most elegant ornament of a French garden. Boyceau praises them as »the low-lying ornamentations of the garden, which can be very graceful, particularly when viewed from an elevated place,« and André Mollet specifies further that they should be designed to be low-lying »so that they can be viewed and considered from the windows [of the château] with more pleasure.«[28]

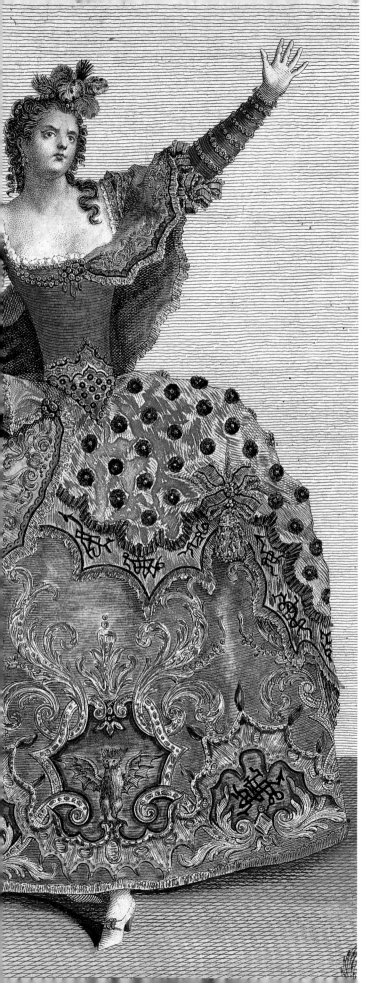

Embroideries provide gardeners with an opportunity to display their virtuosity. Their designs are truly masterpieces of *pourtraiture*, or contour drawing, which Boyceau describes in his treatise on gardening (1638) as »the basis and foundation of all mechanical skills.«[29] The mastery of contour drawing is what enables the gardener to decorate the parterres with ornamental structures that are as complex as they are balanced. Transferring the designs to the grounds requires great technical skill, and André Mollet elaborates on the method to be employed to do so: a plan that is subdivided into a network of squares is transferred to the surface of a bed that has been prepared in the same way, that is, with a grid.[30]

The embroideries of Vaux le Vicomte were reconstructed in the early 1920s by the landscape architect Achille Duchêne. It was, however, a rather free interpretation: originally the tendril ornaments were considerably more delicate, and they were probably filled mainly with yellow sand, contrasting with the charcoal chips, which were used more sparingly; today, however, red brick chips dominate, which produces far too heavy an effect. We must picture the original borders of the beds as having been much narrower, so that the tendril motifs took up considerably more area. Even so, the reconstruction gives some idea of the once virtuosic embroideries that were so typical of the baroque: the ornaments, in limitless variety, recall labyrinths as well as the gala dress or theatrical costumes of the period.

ABOVE:
Detail of the embroidery parterre
in the garden at Vaux

OPPOSITE:
Theater costume for Medea (1749), hand-
colored engraving after Jean-Baptiste Martin

The flower parterre in the garden at Vaux, reconstructed in the year 2000

Although Nicolas Fouquet was unquestionably a lover of flowers — he even had hyacinths, of which he was especially fond, sent from Rome — the garden of Vaux has just one flower parterre, which is, moreover, located on the edge. It was destroyed in the early eighteenth century and planted over with grass, but recently the first attempts at a reconstruction of this parterre have been undertaken. To visitors today it may seem surprising that André Le Nôtre had given flowers such a minor role. Doubtless the gardener's own penchants were other materials and elements, such as lawns, gravel, and water: in this way he freed his creations from the influence of the seasons and gave them an unchanging aspect.

Elaborately ornamented embroidery parterres were, as we have seen, not Le Nôtre's invention, and it may be supposed that the great garden artist considered them old-fashioned and did not hold them in especially high esteem. The famous anecdote about the embroidery parterres of the Tuileries that the duc de Saint-Simon recorded in his memoirs is revealing: »Of parterres he [Le Nôtre] said that they were only for nurses, who, unable to leave their charges, could wander about them with their eyes and admire them from the second floor.«[31] Hence Le Nôtre associated embroideries with the world of women. The same may be said of the flower parterres. Characteristically, the only rich flower ornamentation at Versailles is in the Parterre du Midi, the southern parterre, which could be viewed from the Queen's apartments; the Trianon de Porcelaine, with its legendary splendor of flowers, is clearly a private space intended as a refuge for the king and his lover, Madame de Montespan.

ABOVE:
The Parterre du Midi
(southern parterre) in
the garden at Versailles

OPPOSITE:
The flower parterre in the
garden at Vaux, seen from
the terrace of the château

In the large perspectives that Le Nôtre designed, nature is not blooming but rigorously stylized. In keeping with the value system of French classicism the supreme principle of *raison* dominates here, as it did in literature and architecture. In 1912 the writer Lucien Corpechot characterized Le Nôtre's creations as »gardens of the intelligence.«[32] At Chantilly, for example, the parterres reveal the most rigorous forms imaginable: the flowers, which were originally found only on the borders of the lawn beds, were abandoned entirely as part of a reconstruction in the nineteenth century. Chantilly is dominated by extended, clearly defined planes, particularly in the form of watery surfaces.

André Le Nôtre designed the garden for the Grand Condé, Louis XIV's cousin and a renowned military man. His statue, created in 1690 by Antoine Coysevox, marks the main axis of the parterre. Another statue marks the large terrace, from which a majestic flight of stairs leads down to the parterre. This is an equestrian statue of Connétable Anne de Montmorency that dates only to the nineteenth century. It was a replacement for a very similar, much older statue depicting the Connétable Henri de Montmorency that was destroyed during the revolution. When Le Nôtre redesigned the courtyard of the château and the parterre of the garden he made the equestrian statue of the connétable the linchpin of the whole composition.

Visitors to the garden at Vaux are long captivated by the central axis's impression of infinite depth, which is articulated with particular conciseness in the embroidery parterre. Soon, though, they discover other, unexpected perspectives. The two lateral parterres — the elevated flower parterre to the right and the deeply recessed Parterre de la Couronne on the left — are asymmetrically arranged relative to the central axis, not only with respect to their level but also in their dimensions (see ill. on p. 41). The parterre on the left has a large pool decorated with a gilded crown in the shape of the French royal crown. Originally it shot up jets of water, which also formed a crown. This motif can be interpreted as an homage to Louis XIV, and it is no coincidence that the parterre could be seen from the apartments of the château that were once reserved for the king.

The two lateral parterres create a transverse axis of considerable weight; the Parterre de la Couronne in particular has enormous dimensions and even has its own axis, a line of force that emphasizes its direction toward the hedge and the edge of the forest. This first transverse axis in the garden is contrapuntally related to the main axis and so weighty that it even seems to conflict with it. In the overall composition of the garden, however, the balance stabilized by the central axis is not disturbed; this is one of Le Nôtre's great achievements at Vaux le Vicomte.

ABOVE:
Detail of the state portrait of Louis XIV by
Hyacinthe Rigaud, 1701

OPPOSITE:
View over the Parterre de la Couronne toward
the château at Vaux

Visitors soon discover a second transverse axis; this one is symmetrical to the main axis. On the left, to the west, one finds the Grille d'eau, named for the jets of water that shoot up to form a grille (see Documentation, p. 178). It has a pendant opposite it in the form of an actual grille, behind which the kitchen garden once lay, strictly demarcated from the garden proper. How different from the French garden of the Renaissance, in which fruit trees, vegetables, and fragrant and medicinal herbs all had their place! This is well documented for Diane de Poitiers's garden at Chenonceaux, which was laid out in the 1550s.[33] The wonderful kitchen garden of the château Villandry in the Loire Valley, which was reconstructed at the beginning of the twentieth century, is another example.

ABOVE:
The entrance grille to the former
kitchen garden at Vaux

OPPOSITE:
The kitchen garden at Villandry

The banning of useful trees and plants from the pleasure garden was the clearest sign of a final liberation from agriculture. In 1709 Dezallier d'Argenville categorically called for separate fruit and kitchen gardens, which »ought never to present themselves first to Sight in a handsome Garden.«[34] Jacques Boyceau (1638) had already distinguished between the *jardin de plaisir* (pleasure garden) and the *jardin utile* (kitchen garden), a separation that was taken for granted by Le Nôtre. This did not, however, preclude an artful decoration of the kitchen garden. This was never carried out at Vaux le Vicomte, owing to Nicolas Fouquet's arrest, but at his main residence, Saint-Mandé, there was an extensive kitchen garden that was a masterpiece of ornamental art. It was probably based on designs provided by Le Nôtre (see ill. on p. 44).

Finally, a third transverse axis opens up. It is accentuated by a structure with the strange name Confessionnal, which it acquired at a later date. It contains a grotto and also offers a viewing terrace. The grotto lacks its archetypal element, however: water. That is why it is characterized as the »Grotte Sèche« (dry grotto) on the *Parc de Villars* plan (eighteenth century). The site certainly does not lack water, for a channeled stream runs under the Confessionnal and emerges in the south, at the structure's socle, as a waterfall that flows into the Grand Canal. The stream is buried, so to speak, under the »Dry Grotto.«

From the viewing terrace a feature of the garden is revealed to the visitor that was hidden in the panoramic view from the château: it is evident that the terrain is terraced (see Documentation, pp. 184–85). Terraces are a legacy of the past and evoke memories of Renaissance gardens in Italy, such as the terraces of the Villa Lante, or of French gardens of this era, especially the monumental sequence of terraces at Saint-Germain-en-Laye (circa 1600), which has been preserved in engravings. But, unlike these older layouts, Le Nôtre's terraced steps are concealed: most of them are low, and their retaining walls are masked with clipped hedges. The first transverse axis, with the flower parterre and the Parterre de la Couronne, is also terraced. The spatial plan of the garden — that is, the interlocking of its various levels — thus proves to be highly complex.

ABOVE:
View from the viewing terrace of the Confessionnal toward the garden and château at Vaux

OPPOSITE:
View over the large square pool toward the Confessionnal

In every one of his gardens André Le Nôtre used the existing local irregularities of the terrain to lend variety to his creations. One aspect of this is the contrapuntal interlocking of the central axis with the transverse axes, which was one of his preferred means of design. Each of the transverse axes has its own dynamic, but the harmony of the overall composition is not disturbed. At Sceaux, the residence of the prime minister, Colbert, Le Nôtre responded to the almost chaotic state of the terrain with a plan whose boldness is unique even in his own oeuvre. The main axis, which extends from east to west, is opposed by two subsidiary axes to the south: on one side, the cascade and the large octagonal pool; on the other, the Grand Canal, which is more than half a mile long. These transverse elements are quite autonomous with respect to the central axis, yet they form a unity with it.

André Le Nôtre's predilection for contrapuntal compositions opened a new dimension in the field of garden design. Since Bramante's Belvedere Court at the Vatican, the prototype of the Renaissance garden, the axis of symmetry had always been clearly defined, and even Jacques Boyceau could only imagine a perfect garden as one whose parts were arranged »with symmetry and proper correspondence.«[35] Le Nôtre shrugged off this rule here and introduced to the art of gardening one of the great themes of the baroque age: the conflict between principles that may be opposed but do not destroy one another.

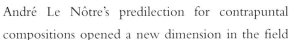

ABOVE:
Plan of the park at Sceaux, engraving,
circa 1730 (north is to the right)

OPPOSITE:
The cascade in the park at Sceaux

»To conclude, it must be noted that none of the soul's means of
knowing the distance of objects will be quite sure [because] rays
from different points of the object differ in the precision with which
they assemble at the back of the eye. The example of *tableaux de perspective*
shows us amply how easy it is to be deceived.«

René Descartes, around 1630

»I prefer to offer a specific demonstration to which I will apply a highly
curious knowledge of the means that the architect of the Trajan Column
in Rome employed to ensure that the figures [. . .] always appear to
be the same size at top as at the bottom, without which [means]
the majority of his work would be invisible to the eye [. . .]. It is by this
means that the Trajan Column is graduated so ingeniously that Art,
compensating for the defects of Nature, makes the most distant parts
as evident to the eye as the closest ones [. . .].«

Roland Fréart de Chantelou, 1663

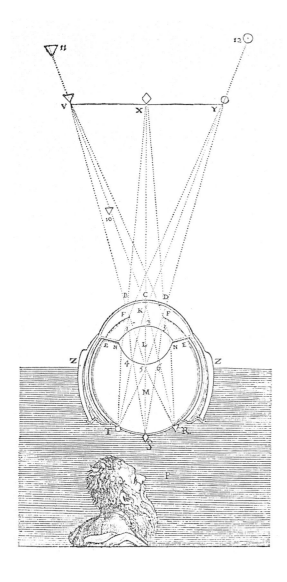

The four pools of the lawn parterre exemplify how artfully Le Nôtre manipulated space. Seen from the château, the grouping of the pools appears to be a well-proportioned ensemble whose parts have equal weight. Le Nôtre achieved this beautiful yet deceptive image by calculating exactly the differences among the pools' sizes when designing them so that the effect of perspective would be »decelerated« — indeed, eliminated completely. Only by examining them more closely will the visitor appreciate that they are in fact far from one another and of completely different dimensions. The surface of the water in the square pool is eight times as great as that of the round pool that lies closer to the château, and the distance between the two pools is 720 feet.

The other elements of the garden are also larger the farther they are from the château. For example, the lawn parterre, where the square pool is found, is three times as large as the embroidery parterre immediately in front of the château. The sculptures also vary greatly in size. The atlantes of the grotto are three times as tall as the groups of figures on the château's terrace; the statue of Hercules, which is even more distant, is twice as tall as the atlantes, if the pedestal is included.

In this André Le Nôtre was using the method now known as *perspective ralentie*, or decelerated perspective, in which the scale of things is adjusted to the eye of the beholder. This method had already been used in several French gardens in the 1630s, like Richelieu, for example; it is, however, not mentioned in Jacques Boyceau's *Traité du jardinage* of 1638. The only possible evidence of it would be the recommendation expressed there to make the width of an allée proportional to its length, but ultimately this is not convincing.[36] When Boyceau wrote of the harmonious composition of a garden, however, he had in mind above all the division of the planes into clear, geometric forms, and it is the outline of the garden that is intended to demonstrate the beauty of proportions: the »decorum of all the parts.«[37] Boyceau's statements about the education of a gardener are revealing in this context. He places a high value on the study of geometry: »he must ascend to geometry, fundamental for all plans, departments, measures, and alignments.«[38] The viewer, however, will experience the geometry of a garden from a perspective that distorts greatly, and Boyceau hardly takes this fact into account at all.

In his treatise Jacques Boyceau thus still persisted in the classical geometric composition of a garden. Soon, however, *perspective ralentie* would be developed by André Mollet, in his treatise *Le jardin de plaisir*, published in 1651. Mollet gives the following advice to gardeners who would like to employ his designs for parterres: »to that end, the first thing to note is that the parterres furthest from view must be laid out in greater volume than those closer in order to appear more agreeable to the eye and better proportioned.«[39] To clarify his intentions, Mollet presented several plates of such parterres, with the back beds significantly larger than the front ones.[40]

André Le Nôtre certainly picked up on such ideas, but he developed them so rigorously and on such a grander scale that his gardens can scarcely be compared to those of the preceding era. The artist exploited all the possibilities of trompe l'oeil that *perspective ralentie* offered to counteract the laws of optical distortion to which visitors to his expansive garden spaces are necessarily subjected. In doing so he took a tried and true method from painting and graphic arts and made it productive for the art of the garden. In her analysis of the large axis of the garden of Versailles, Marguerite Charageat made reference to the »anamorphic compositions« that were discussed in certain circles of artists and scholars in the 1630s and 1640s.[41] Anamorphoses are highly distorted planar projections of objects or figures. When such »decomposed« images are viewed at a very acute angle, the objects or figures appear to have their correct proportions.

Saint Francis of Paula, anamorphic mural
by Emmanuel Maignan in the monastery
SS. Trinità dei Monti, Rome, 1642

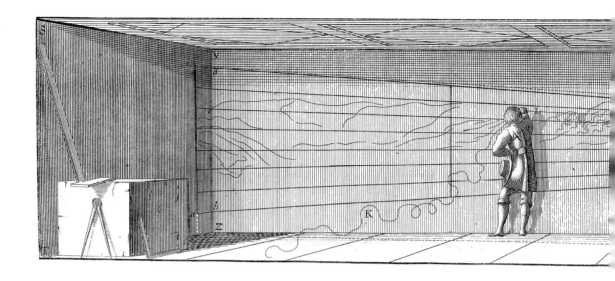

Making an anamorphic mural (above) and
demonstration of an anamorphosis (below),
engravings by Jean-François Niceron, 1646
and 1638

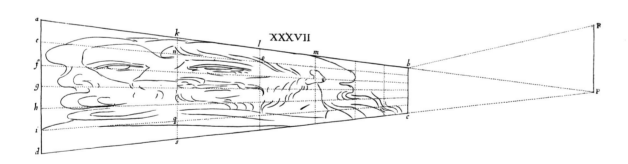

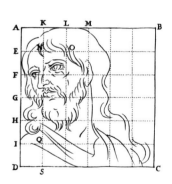

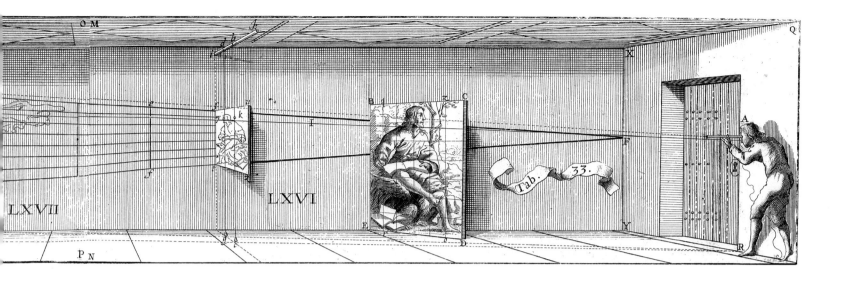

Anamorphic compositions were particularly esteemed in the circles of the Order of Minims. One can still see today a masterpiece of this genre in the monastery of SS. Trinità dei Monti in Rome: in a long corridor there is a mural painted by the monk Emmanuel Maignan that shows Saint Francis of Paula in a landscape with the Bay of Messina.

Similar anamorphic frescoes could once be seen in Paris: namely, in a monastery that belonged to the Order of Minims, near the Place Royale, today's Place des Vosges.[42] These frescoes were the work of the monk Jean-François Niceron, who was an important scholar. Niceron became widely known for a work he published in 1638, *La perspective curieuse*, in which the phenomenon of anamorphoses is explained in detail and illustrated.[43] In the book Niceron elucidated his theses using only figurative depictions but the frescoes he painted in the Minim monastery also depict landscapes that were deformed in the same way as his figures of saints.[44]

André Le Nôtre certainly knew Niceron's frescoes and theses, and even if it is not possible to prove a direct influence on his work, they presumably encouraged him to provide a decisive solution to one of the greatest problems that confronted him: namely, the fact that the surfaces of a garden are perceived from an extremely acute angle of vision. This problem becomes all the more volatile the more extensive the garden is. At Vaux le Vicomte Le Nôtre faced the challenge of organizing a space with a depth of more than half a mile. In accomplishing this task, he was probably inspired by Niceron's theoretical reflections. In his study *Mirrors of Infinity* Allen S. Weiss has rightly characterized the overall composition of the garden at Vaux as an anamorphosis.[45]

At Vaux le Vicomte, as in Le Nôtre's other gardens, the elements of the landscape appear to the viewer as if they were coordinated in harmonious proportions to one another. But appearances deceive. The most famous example of such trompe l'oeil effects is the Grand Canal at Versailles. The visitor sees three pools that appear to be the same size; in reality, however, their dimensions range widely: the furthest pool is three times as long as the first one (see ill. on p. 143). What the viewer sees is thus based on an illusion, that is, on a purely subjective perception that does not correspond to objective circumstances. This play with the difference between illusion and reality is one of the most important features of baroque art.

Illusion triumphs in the gardens of André Le Nôtre. This is an almost heretical break with the humanist ideal of the *divina proportione* to which so many Renaissance gardens were indebted. Such gardens are dominated by the elementary forms of geometry: the circle and the square. The most beautiful example is the large parterre at the Villa Lante. Its geometric pattern resembles that of the tile floors seen in so many Renaissance paintings; it was used almost obsessively by artists as a motif that enabled them to structure painted spaces as clearly as possible.

LEFT:
The Villa at Castello near Florence, painting by Giusto Utens, 1598 (detail)

OPPOSITE:
The large parterre of the Villa Lante in Bagnaia, near Viterbo

92

View of an ideal city, painting by an anonymous
Italian master, late fifteenth century

Visitors to the garden of Vaux le Vicomte experience another illusionistic effect after walking around the large square pool at the end of the lawn parterre and turning back toward the château: the whole building is reflected in the water, even though it is more than a quarter mile distant. This is the first *miroir d'eau* in the history of the art of gardening: water used as a mirror, one of Le Nôtre's inventions. The distance between the château and the pool seems to have been neutralized by means of a magic spell, but all the artist did to achieve it was apply a law of optics: for the viewer, the object's angle of incidence has to correspond to the angle of reflection of the mirror image. The Parterre de la Couronne provides the viewer with a similar experience: here the château seems to be reflected in the large, oval pool, but this time in an oblique view (see ill. on p. 77).

The square pool offers yet another optical illusion. Although the grotto seems to rise up immediately behind the pool, it is not reflected in it at all (see ill. on pp. 98–99). The further the visitor moves along the central axis into the depths of the garden, the more unreal the composition of the surface of the water and the grotto, flanked by stairs and ramps, becomes — a coup of optical seduction. The architectural elements present themselves in an impressive concentration, contrasting with the still surface of the water; and the steps and ramps, with their cones of yew trees, develop a dynamic of forms that is not found anywhere else in the garden. This perfect composition is, however, purely illusory: in reality the surface of the water and the grotto do not belong together at all: they are widely separated. Nevertheless, the near and the distant seem to meet here; the wide space between reveals itself to visitors only when they have reached the edge of the parterre and discovered the canal.

View over the large square pool toward
the château at Vaux

This fascinating area of the garden is where Le Nôtre undertook the most earthwork: on the one hand, there are ditches near the canal; on the other, aggradations at the end of the parterre. This enabled him to obscure the distance between the grotto and the pool — which is more than 220 yards — and produce the astonishing illusion that the building and the surface of the water touch. The optical effect is similar to that produced by a telescope, and it is achieved precisely by means of the artificial contours of the terrain. In his calculations Le Nôtre followed methods used in building fortresses: the ramps and the terraces on both sides of the grotto are directly related to military architecture. Le Nôtre minimized the martial effect by masking the retaining walls with hedges and planting the terraces with yews pruned to form cones.

View over the large square pool toward the grotto, with its steps and ramps, in the garden at Vaux

»Beyond the large square pool one descends further, and one sees something completely surprising. Indeed, the imagination cannot conceive anything so grand, so agreeable, so magnificent [. . .].«

Madeleine de Scudéry, 1661

»[. . .] I know the pleasure I would have given Your Majesty, and I would have had the honor of directing your attention to the beautiful places and hearing from you that it is a beautiful thing of nature to see a river descend as an astounding waterfall and create the beginning of an endless canal. There is no need to ask whence the water of this canal comes. Forgive me, I would have become carried away about many things, having directed everything down to the last allée and the entrance when one leaves the forest to arrive on the terrace [and discover] what one can see there at a glance from the edge of the grand staircase.«

André Le Nôtre, 1698*

»[. . .] the rules for revealing and spiriting away were a marvelous success at Vaux le Vicomte, but they were by no means observed consistently at Versailles.«

Achille Duchêne (1866–1947)

---

* In 1698 the Earl of Portland visited several famous gardens in France;
Le Nôtre would have liked to demonstrate to him the beauties of his own works.

The low–lying area that is found at the end of the parterre reveals to the viewer another transverse axis that was completely hidden until then: the Grand Canal, which is fed by the Anqueil River. The dimensions — 930 yards long and 38 yards wide — and the large trees that border this dammed waterway recall the shipping canals that were then being built throughout the kingdom, such as the Canal du Midi, which was begun in 1666. Le Nôtre knew this area well, as is demonstrated by the large canal in the garden of Chantilly, which is adapted to the terrain with astonishing technical skill.[46]

The channeling of water was a familiar theme of the French garden since the Renaissance — for example, at the Maison-Blanche in Gaillon or the château of Fleury-en-Bière. From 1607 to 1609 Henry IV had a canal excavated in the park of Fontainebleau whose dimensions — three-quarters of a mile long and 43 yards wide — exceed those of the Grand Canal at Vaux le Vicomte. In Tanlay in Burgundy the architect Pierre Le Muet had a canal excavated in the 1640s that was also of considerable size: 575 yards long and 26 yards wide.

PREVIOUS PAGE:
Term in the Parterre de la Couronne of the garden at Vaux

RIGHT:
The Grand Canal at Vaux, with the sculptures of the
Quatre parties du monde (late nineteenth century)

What distinguishes the Grand Canal of Vaux le Vicomte from all its predecessors is the way it is integrated into the terrain: although it is hidden from view for so long, it nevertheless represents the most impressive of the garden's transverse axes. In the middle section, which lies precisely opposite the château, the dammed waterway has none of the features of a typical canal and partakes of the spacious, complex structure of reflecting water surfaces and bright, gravel-covered terraces. This composition is one of the most important in Le Nôtre's oeuvre, and it recalls one of his later masterpieces: the extended parterre of Chantilly and its reflecting pools.

In order to hide the canal from the viewer's gaze for so long, Le Nôtre had to manipulate substantially the terrain, which dropped gently toward the Anqueil River: the high aggradation at the end of the lawn parterre created a prominent step in the terrain, and this is what conceals the canal. Vaux le Vicomte was André Le Nôtre's first experience with the interplay of hiding and revealing, and it was accomplished so magnificently that it is proper to speak of a turning point in the art of the garden. The landscape was no longer conceived statically but in such a way that transformations analogous to the stage decorations of the baroque theater could occur.

Such interplays of hiding and revealing are found in other genres of seventeenth-century art as well, such as in the paintings of Diego Velázquez, Jan Vermeer, or Jacob van Ruisdael. These painters deliberately directed the viewer's attention to spaces that were hidden in the composition of their paintings and could only be surmised. One famous example of this typically baroque artistic approach is Velázquez's painting *The Family of Philip IV* (known as *Las Meninas*, 1656): in it the king and queen appear only as a reflection in a mirror in the background, while the space in which they stand is invisible; the depiction of this space on the painter's canvas is also hidden. Another important example is Poussin's self-portrait in the Louvre, in which the room is obstructed by large canvases; only one of these canvases depicts anything, yet it is highly fragmented and mysterious.

ABOVE:
The Stairway of a Hundred Steps, which connects to the western wing of the Orangerie at Versailles

OPPOSITE:
Nicolas Poussin, self-portrait, 1650

EFFIGIES NICOLA POVSSINI ANDEL
YENSIS PICTORIS ANNO ÆTATIS 56
ROMÆ ANNO IVBILEI
1650.

Le Nôtre would employ this interplay of hiding and revealing on a massive scale at Versailles. A mile and a quarter of the central axis, which is nearly two miles long, are hidden from a viewer standing at the château. The same is true of the transverse axis: only when visitors reach the edge of the Parterre du Midi do they see the Orangerie and its parterre, far below this terrace, having seen only the Swiss Guard Pool in the distance at first. At Chantilly these surprises are even greater: as one approaches the terrace with the equestrian statue of the connétable, one does not see the garden at all at first, so that it is all the more astonishing when one arrives on the terrace (see ill. on pp. 74, 75).

ABOVE:
The parterre of the Orangerie and the Swiss
Guard Pool in the garden at Versailles

OPPOSITE:
The Parterre du Midi (below) and the Swiss
Guard Pool (above) in the garden at Versailles

In her description of the garden at Vaux, Madeleine de Scudéry attributes particular importance to the Grand Canal, and she describes the unexpected view as an unusual experience: »Behind the large square pool one descends further, and one sees something completely surprising. Indeed, the imagination cannot conceive anything so grand, so agreeable, so magnificent; Nature, as omnipotent as she is, cannot produce anything so beautiful; and Art, which often prides itself on imitating her, of surpassing her sometimes, and embellishing her always, could never create anything this marvelous. Thus one can say that what one sees here is a masterpiece of Art and Nature joined together.«[47]

The grotto is the most important structure in the garden; in the seventeenth century it was considered the main attraction of Vaux le Vicomte, admired by travelers from all over Europe. The overall design is by André Le Nôtre, while the sculptures were executed after drawings by Charles Le Brun. Grottoes are part of the traditional inventory of a garden, and they had been highly esteemed in France since the Renaissance, particularly in the form of walls with arcades, behind which there were spaces designed to look like caves. Not infrequently the most important places in the gardens were retained for such structures; this was the case at Meudon and, even more impressively, at Saint-Germain-en-Laye. At Vaux le Vicomte the grotto offers a flat facade, and it differs so greatly from the older grottoes that were meant to evoke caves that contemporaries had difficulty calling it a grotto. In his poem *Le songe de Vaux* Jean de La Fontaine speaks of a »projecting structure opposite the cascade,«[48] while Madeleine de Scudéry describes the grotto in rather long-winded fashion as »a terrace with a balustrade supported by six architectural terms.«[49]

ABOVE:
Stairway next to the grotto at Vaux

OPPOSITE:
The grotto at Vaux and its reflection in the pool of the Grand Canal

The formal relationship of the grotto at Vaux to the later designs for the Orangerie at Versailles and the Grand Degré at Chantilly, where Le Nôtre was also involved in the planning, have rightly been emphasized. Both of the latter are considered perfect examples of the *style classique*.[50] Thus, when several authors describe the grotto at Vaux as the model for the other two, they are attributing this formal characteristic to it as well. According to other authors, however, the grotto at Vaux reveals picturesque traits or even a »rustic mannerism,« as Jean-Pierre Babelon writes[51] — a conclusion that is not justified. Certainly the grotto has several traditional rustic features, like the rusticated ashlar, but these elements are subordinated to the severe, and hence classical, character of the overall architecture.

The grotto (above) and the large stairway (opposite) in the garden at Chantilly

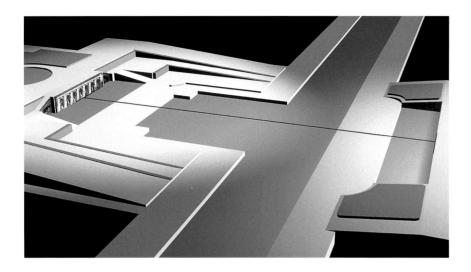

Opposite the grotto there is a cascade: a long wall, reinforced by pillars, which is flanked by ramps and steps. These two structures have very different weights within the overall concept of the garden: while the cascade is kept from the viewer's gaze entirely as long as they remain on the parterre level, the grotto is always present as a dominant accent in the central perspective of the garden.

When viewing the cascade wall from the banks of the canal, it looks as if it were the foundation for the esplanade on which the parterres spread toward the château. Opposite the cascade, and on the same level, lies the grotto. Standing at the château, however, one has the impression that the grotto is on a higher »level,« as if it were standing on the upper edge of the cascade — which is otherwise hidden — and were raised above the esplanade with the parterres (see ill. on p. 87). The mystery can only be solved when the viewer has examined the canal area more closely. The two structures are about 220 yards apart, and this distance, precisely calculated by Le Nôtre, puts the upper edge of the cascade at the lower edge of the grotto when seen from the viewer's angle. This is among the most brilliant mathematical calculations in the history of landscaping.

Yet another feature of the grotto shows how perfectly it is integrated into the main perspective of the garden: the structure manages to dominate the perspective without interrupting it, because it is incorporated into the hillside such that it does not rise above it. This demonstrates again how precisely Le Nôtre calculated the contours of the terrain when planning the garden.

ABOVE:
Demonstration of the viewing angle at which the grotto at Vaux is seen by a viewer from the château (see also illustration on pp. 98–99)

OPPOSITE:
The cascade, the parterres, and the château at Vaux

»You need not be aggrieved that the palace where we are [the grotto] offers less
pleasure to the eyes than does the one that looks over it [the château]. One might
say, in truth, that its allées [the ramps] are so beautiful that it would be quite
awkward to add anything to them; one may also say that its face has a certain
grandness and nobility to it: but the niches they have placed there have not yet
been filled with anything but very dry rocks [. . .].«
Jean de La Fontaine, circa 1660

»I imagine, in my dream, two ambassadors are sent to Monsieur Fouquet
by the god Neptune, to offer him all the treasures of the sea, some
petrifaction, all sorts of coral, some conches, so that Monsieur Fouquet
might have been able to decorate certain rocks that are in an
architectural projection opposite the cascade at Vaux.«
Jean de La Fontaine, circa 1660

»Folio 14 contains the account of Monsieur Blanchard, sculptor, and [it is]
indicated that he was paid everything he was owed up to January 14, 1659 /
And then an agreement was made with him by Monsieur Le Nôtre
for the thirty animals of rocks [. . .].«
Archives of Olivier Lefèvre d'Ormesson, after 1661

PREVIOUS PAGE:
Detail of the grotto at Vaux

ABOVE:
Perspective of the Grand Canal at Vaux
toward the west

OPPOSITE:
The Allée d'eau in the garden at Versailles

At Vaux le Vicomte, as in all the gardens before it, water plays a key role. This is clear as soon as one approaches the château, when the moats are seen, as their revetments are decorated with wall fountains. Even in the main courtyard there is — quite unusually — water present in the form of pools on the lateral terraces. The pools in the parterres are both numerous and varied in form; there are also small canals that separate the parterres. The Grille d'eau that forms the western termination of the middle transverse axis was admired at the time, and even more so the Allée d'eau, now lost, that provided an important accent in the axis of the lawn parterre and hence in the garden's central axis. An anonymous chronicler of the fête of 1661 remarked of this feature: »One walks between two walls of water,«[52] and Madeleine de Scudéry praised the magical effect of this »crystal balustrade.«[53] The Allée d'eau at Vaux was the model for the one at Versailles.

ABOVE:
The Avenue of a Hundred Fountains in the garden
of the Villa d'Este in Tivoli, east of Rome

OPPOSITE:
Detail of the cascade wall in the garden at Vaux

The grotto and the cascade are particularly impressive displays of the wealth of water that dominates at Vaux and is a condition of all great waterworks. The latter were the primary criteria for judging a garden's quality in the seventeenth century. On the occasion of the fête of 1661 King Louis XIV and the members of his retinue visited Fouquet's garden and admired this »abundance of water.« The magnificence of the waterworks occasioned the anonymous author of the fête chronicle to remark »that Tivoli and Frascati and all the beautiful, magnificent, and surprising things that Italy boasts of possessing [. . .] have nothing to compare to Vaux.«[54]

Madeleine de Scudéry also praised the variety of water, and described with great accuracy the garden's artful waterworks. In her novel *Clélie* she begins the chapter on »Valterre« — her fictive name for Vaux — with a dialogue between two actors, one of whom confuses the name Valterre with that of the »famous city« of Volterra. But what at first appears to be a simple misunderstanding turns out to have a meaning: »because this city has so much water that there is no gate or square that does not have a fountain, so the conformity between the waters led to the resemblance in name.«[55] Both Madeleine de Scudéry's novel and the fête chronicle echo France's cultural rivalry with Italy, and Vaux le Vicomte is praised as a place that surpasses all others.

In contrast to grottoes, cascades do not appear in French gardens until relatively late. One searches in vain for them in the inventory of the elements of an ideal garden that André Mollet compiled.[56] One of the earliest examples is the relatively small Gondi cascade at Saint-Cloud, which was built between 1625 and 1644 but has not survived.[57] It was clearly the model for the cascade at Vaux. The cascade at Liancourt, however, which was completed before 1637, is only comparable to Vaux's in that it adapted to a terrace in the garden.[58] The cascade was certainly an important element of the French garden, but not a dominant one; this is true even of the bizarre water stairway in Cardinal Richelieu's garden at Rueil, which was once much admired.[59]

The cascade wall at Vaux

The cascades recalled Italy — even more than the grottoes did. In the gardens of the Aldobrandini and Torlonia villas in Frascati the spectacularly designed cascades were made the focus. In Le Nôtre's gardens, by contrast, the cascade, with its rustic reminiscences and its crash of falling water, could never occupy a central place, as it would not suit the classical configuration of a main perspective, which was dominated by the severe rules of order. Although the cascade of Sceaux, an enormous stairway of water, is given great weight, it does not lie in the central perspective of the garden but on a transverse axis (see ill. on p. 82). At Versailles such cascades were constructed in, or in some cases merely planned for, the hidden bosquets.[60] At Vaux le Vicomte, Le Nôtre made use of the very tumultuous contours of the terrain to integrate the cascade into the ensemble of the garden in such a way that it only occasionally enters the visitor's field of vision.

ABOVE:
A bosquet, known as the Salle de Bal
(ballroom), in the garden at Versailles

OPPOSITE:
Detail of one of the candelabras that
decorate the Salle de Bal bosquet in
the garden at Versailles

Whereas the water in the parterres is evident only in strictly stylized forms, in the area of the canal it is freed to rush along; here it produces »such a grand and beautiful noise that everyone thinks it is the throne of Neptune.«[61] At the cascade this element is unleashed, pouring out of grotesque masks. The execution of the structure — with its rough-hewn stones — suits this well. The wall of the grotto opposite gives a very different impression. The only features of the latter that suggest wild nature are the rock fountains and the miniature grottoes to the side, which are decorated with icicles and provide space for the river gods. These motifs seem secondary to the dignified forms of the overall architectural design, whose masonry is meticulous throughout. Here there is no din of water, just a restrained lapping. Finally, another important difference vis-à-vis the cascade is that the grotto is nearly always in shadow and is brushed by the rays of the sun only shortly before sundown.

The sculptures of the grotto, designed by Charles Le Brun and executed by Mathieu Lespagnandel, underline the dignified character of the structure. In the two grotto caves there are monumental figures of river gods. The pose of the river god Tiber recalls works by Michelangelo, especially the allegorical figure of Night in the Medici Chapel in Florence. Madeleine de Scudéry accurately described Tiber's expression as "melancholic," and she offered an explanation: »because he is angry that he has been outdone by the local river god who is seen represented with a gay and joyous air on the far side.«[62]

ABOVE:
The statue of Tiber on the right side of the grotto at Vaux

OPPOSITE:
Atlantes and rock fountains of the grotto at Vaux

Statue of Anqueil on the left side
of the grotto at Vaux

The seven niches of the grotto contain strangely stylized fountains consisting of artificial crags that look like petrified water. They are framed by eight atlantes. These figures appear to be caught in the net formed by the joints of the rusticated ashlar of the walls. The atlantes stand as pendants to the eight stone guards who parade along the entrance grille of the forecourt. Their faces reveal a rich spectrum of characters and even express violent emotions. We should recall that the atlantes were designed by Charles Le Brun, who achieved fame through his numerous studies on the expression of the passions. The aquatic plants that crown their heads are meant to suggest that these athletic creatures come from Neptune's realm. An extravagant fountain with sculptures of the sea god and his Tritons was originally planned for the large basin toward which the canal stretches out in front of the grotto, but this project was not realized.

The realm of the river gods offers a particularly subtle surprise for visitors to the garden. Seen from a distance the grotto appears to have a facade of rough stone and the niches appear to be filled with meticulously executed sculptures. In reality, however, the situation is reversed. This is one of many illusionistic effects that Le Nôtre staged at Vaux.

LEFT AND OPPOSITE:
The atlantes of the grotto at Vaux

In this realm reserved for river gods and nymphs Le Nôtre permitted himself bizarreries that he deliberately avoided elsewhere in the garden. When visitors observe the reflections in the water and then fixate again on the wall of the grotto, strange, ambiguous figures reveal themselves in the rock fountains. Are they monsters or enormous antic masks? Even in their original state these figures were only suggested, but today, after many restorations, they are even more difficult to recognize. A few historical documents demonstrate that the obscure monsters were identified by attentive observers of earlier epochs, such as Dezallier d'Argenville, who mentioned the »animals« of the grotto in his *Voyage pittoresque des environs de Paris* (1762 edition). It is bizarre that they are more easily recognized in their reflections in the water than in the rock fountains themselves.

Curiosities of this form were among the greatest attractions that gardens of the Renaissance and early baroque had to offer. One thinks, for example, of the grotto at Gaillon, the so-called Maison-Blanche, which precedes the one at Vaux le Vicomte by about a hundred years: here visitors were surprised by satyrs in obscene poses. In the garden at Rueil, which was designed around 1635 for Cardinal Richelieu, there was an admirable grotto with a grotesque portal that Élie Brackenhoffer's travelogue of 1644 – 45 described as follows: »a large open mouth [. . .]. The head is made of beautiful stone, it has large ears, an immense throat; it is terrifying from afar.«[63] Another grotto in the same garden had shells in the form of satyrs and other wild creatures.

LEFT AND OPPOSITE:
Rock fountains in the niches of the grotto at Vaux

The wild creatures that are nested in the grotto of Vaux le Vicomte recall the primal, untamed forces of nature, but this illusion remains discreet and is almost lost within the larger framework of the art of the garden, which is dominated by the mode of civilized order. Even the immediate vicinity of the grotto, which consists of stairs, ramps, and terraces, bears the stamp of this order, a triumph of Le Nôtre's art for designing spaces using large dimensions and severe forms. The impression of size is reinforced by four groups of sculpture that mark the prelude to the ramps on both sides of the grotto: »on large pedestals one sees depictions of the various parts of the world, holding in their hands the precious things from the countries they represent, presenting them as a tribute to show that the whole world has contributed to the decoration of this place.«[64] This description by Madeleine de Scudéry is fiction. The sculptures did not yet exist in her day, but were only planned; they were not executed until the end of the nineteenth century as part of the great restoration campaign.

LEFT AND OPPOSITE:
Retaining walls and ramps
adjacent to the grotto at Vaux

Stairs and terraces adjacent to the grotto at Vaux

»On folio 12 it is indicated that Monsieur Poissant, sculptor, was paid for all his works up through the end of 1659. / That he concluded a contract to deliver the plaster model for the large figure of Hercules that he has brought from Rome and to repair something in exchange for 3,000 livres for himself and 7,000 livres for Monsieur Delaporte [. . .].«
Archives of Olivier Lefèvre d'Ormesson, after 1661

»[Further] I made the model for the pedestal of the large Hercules, including the steps around it, following the orders of Monsieur Le Brun.«
Jacques Prou, circa 1661

»In the room in which the painter Monsieur Le Brun was lodged [. . .] a wax model of a Hercules [. . .].«
Inventory of Vaux, September 1661

When visitors climb up to the statue of Hercules that crowns the panorama of the garden, they experience the biggest surprise of their tour. From that height, looking back, the garden is seen in a perspective that differs utterly from that seen from the château. No longer does the central axis draw one's gaze into the depths; now the horizontal gradation of the terraces dominates. In addition, the pools, the gravel paths, and the lawns seem to form a tight network and produce an extremely pure composition of lines and planes.

The château also seems to have transformed as well, relative to its appearance when seen from close up. Now we understand why the facades of the outbuildings are so carefully executed — specifically, in that combination of sandstone and bricks that had been so popular in France since the Renaissance. At first these outbuildings, far from the château, appear to be of lesser significance; looking back from the statue of Hercules, however, this impression turns out to be wrong, for now the distance between the château and the outbuildings seems so slight that they give the impression of being a single structure of considerable size. The chronicler of the fête of August 17, 1661, noted this: »I do not wish to leave this site without pointing out to you that one has seen here the most beautiful perspective in the world; the château, which is [only] one of the beautiful buildings one sees, is the attention getter therein, together with the courtyards, which, even though fairly far apart, seem to be connected to the château, making it appear to be more extended.«[65]

PREVIOUS PAGE AND RIGHT:
Statue of Hercules, view looking back over
the garden toward the château at Vaux

The garden at Vaux with the château and its outbuildings, seen from the statue of Hercules

Seen from the château, the garden appears to the visitor as if it were seen through a wide-angle lens. Conversely, the view from the height — that is, from the Hercules — is like a telescopic view. The effect of vanishing perspective is extremely decelerated; the zones of space appear to have been pulled together. Le Nôtre was able to create this astonishing vista because the space of the garden is so deep. The lawn parterre is one-third of a mile from the viewer and the château is more than half a mile. At Versailles, Le Nôtre would be commissioned to use his art to organize a space that was nearly two miles deep. There he would create the famous concluding prospect whose fascinating effect is based on the planes and volumes seeming so highly compressed. On the horizon one sees two poplars that stand out from the sky as slender silhouettes; they were planted in Napoleon's day as replacements for the elms that originally stood there in the same arrangement. But appearances deceive: in reality the two poplars are the beginning of an allée that is nearly two hundred meters long. This allée was destroyed during the storm of December 26, 1999.

ABOVE:
The Grand Canal at Versailles, after the great
storm of 1999

OPPOSITE:
The poplar allée at the end of the large axis
at Versailles, before it was destroyed in the
great storm of 1999

The statue of Hercules was not erected until the end of the nineteenth century. Although it was planned in Fouquet's day, his arrest prevented it from being realized. This ancient hero is present not only in the garden but also in the decorations of the château's interior. The ceiling of the Salon d'Hercule, the antechamber of Fouquet's apartment, has a painting by Charles Le Brun, *L'apothéose d'Hercule*. The hero represents the victory of reason, because — as Madeleine de Scudéry had already observed — he controls the fiery horses »who by their impulsive action teach us that here they represent the passions, which, despite their violence, are subdued before Reason.«[66]

The colossal statue at the end of the garden was — like the allegory in the château — intended as a flattering allusion to the owner. In both places the ancient hero figures as a pioneer of civilization, because »it is he who clears out nature for human habitation and in accordance with a human sense of order.«[67] Fouquet was including himself among the descendants of this illustrious ancestor. This had already been noted by Madeleine de Scudéry, when she described the colossal statue as if it had in fact been executed and put in place: »And as if to mark that this is the final piece of this grand and beautiful work, they placed nearby [near the fountain called La Gerbe] a beautiful figure of Hercules resting after all the labors that one sees depicted in relief on the pedestal.«[68]

ABOVE:
L'apothéose d'Hercule, detail from the ceiling painting
by Charles Le Brun in the Salon d'Hercule of the
château at Vaux, circa 1660

OPPOSITE:
Project for the statue of Hercules at Vaux, detail from
the engraving *Vue et perspective de la grotte et d'une
partie du canal* by Israël Silvestre, before 1660

As we have mentioned, Fouquet's arrest prevented the realization of the statue, but thanks to Israël Silvestre's engraving *Vue et perspective de la grotte . . .* we know what it was supposed to look like. The engraving shows the statue only schematically, but it is clear that it is a copy of the Farnese Hercules. Silvestre's reproduction is laterally inverted relative to the original. In the original the hero is resting on his club with his body leaning to the left. The inversion of this pose at Vaux le Vicomte is significant. The figure there is facing east, corresponding with a striking feature of the garden: namely, its weighting to one side, that is, the emphasis on the east side that results from the Parterre de la Couronne, the Grille d'eau, and the Confessionnal. When the statue was realized toward the end of the nineteenth century, a faithful copy of the ancient original was chosen.

The decision to terminate the large perspective of the garden with a colossal statue based on the Farnese Hercules was a fortuitous one. Recall Bernini's remark about this ancient sculpture, as passed down by Chantelou: »He praised it, observing that it was by an excellent Greek artist but that it had been made to be seen at a certain distance, and that where it is placed now, the further one moves away, the more admirable it appears.«[69]

ABOVE:
The eastern side of the garden at Vaux

OPPOSITE:
The statue of Hercules at Vaux, projected circa 1660 and executed around 1890

»When Their Majesties had supped, everyone hurried to take seats in the comedy. The theater was set up in the high forest, with many jets of water, several niches, and other pleasant things. And the introduction was by Molière, who said to the king that he could not entertain His Majesty, his comrades being sick, unless some other aid were to arrive. At that instant a rock opened up and [the dancer] Béjart came out, dressed as a goddess. She recited a prologue to the king on all his virtues [. . .] and in his name she commanded the terms to walk and trees to speak, and immediately Louis made the trees move and the trees speak.«

Anonymous chronicler of the fête at Vaux on August 17, 1661

»As soon as the king arrived in Nantes, he wanted to carry out his design against the superintendent, who had undertaken the voyage while sick with swamp fever, but his reason was stronger, so that he followed the king, because he had great plans to secure his fortune and his favor that he wanted to bring to a conclusion. His high-flying thoughts caused him to fall into the precipice, and the excess of his ambition was the source of his misfortunes. The king, who knew that he had purchased nearly all the men of the court, did not dare entrust his captain of the guard to arrest him: for this he chose d'Artagnan, a creature of the late Cardinal [Mazarin], who commanded his musketeers.«

Françoise Langlois de Motteville, 1660s

Nicolas Fouquet organized a fête for a viewing of his château and garden on August 17, 1661, although it had, of course, been ordered by Louis XIV, who chose the date personally. The king had already visited Vaux in 1660 and had had an opportunity to see Fouquet's new residence, which was then still under construction. The château and garden must have left him with mixed feelings, as his own residences seemed old-fashioned and even shabby by comparison.

By August 1661 construction was nearly completed. The superintendent received the king, the queen mother, and a large part of the courtly retinue. Later reports of the fête exaggerated the number of guests terribly; in fact, there might have been about a thousand. Molière's play *Les fâcheux* was performed, in which the writer himself appeared. The stage was constructed above the Grille d'eau. An actress recited the prologue, in which the king's virtues and deeds were praised; in the name of the king she ordered the terms to walk and the trees to speak.[70]

The château was illuminated by candles that were lined up closely in the window niches. The grotto and its ramps were also lit, forming an »amphitheater of fire.« Fireworks concluded the fête. According to an eyewitness, a million rockets rose from the cupola of the château and went down beyond the Grand Canal, spanning the entire garden with a »vault of fire.«[71]

The main attractions, however, were the château and the garden. The king scrutinized this total work of art attentively — admiring and enraged at once. The elimination of his subject was a fait accompli. »Inexorable, the king's resentment: Louis XIV against Fouquet, it is the poor man against the rich man,« wrote Paul Morand.[72] The superintendent, wrapped up in his dream, had lost any sense of the reality of the world at court, with its strict rules of self-control; he had committed a faux pas. Voltaire would later comment: »On August 17, at six in the evening, Fouquet was the king of France; at two in the morning he was nothing anymore.«[73]

ABOVE AND OPPOSITE:
The château and garden at Vaux,
illuminated by oil lamps

The fête of August 17 was certainly one factor, but it was not the deciding factor in the superintendent's fall. It has been shown the preparations for Fouquet's elimination had been begun some three months earlier: he had been made responsible for the disorder that reigned in the state's finances and been accused of embezzling funds. The extent to which this was merely a slanderous campaign is still debated today.

A key role in the Fouquet affair was played by Jean-Baptiste Colbert, and any judgment about the proceedings requires that his personality and political objectives be evaluated. What motives were the deciding factors in his relentless attitude toward the superintendent? The opinions of historians are divided. Jean-Christian Petitfils conjectures, cautiously, that he was guided not by personal objectives but by farsighted ones: »Colbert wanted to oppose the ›maxim of order‹ to that of ›disorder,‹ represented by his enemy.«[74] Indeed, the position of power that the superintendent occupied as the mediator between the king and the financiers could represent a threat to the ruler. Inès Murat is of that view: »Colbert rightly saw the superintendent's function as a symbol of the state's nonexistence in the area of finances and thus as a symbol for the fragility of royal power.«[75] The economic historian Daniel Dessert is of the opposite opinion: »In every respect Jean-Baptiste [Colbert] built his reputation on the rubble of that of Nicolas [Fouquet].«[76] Dessert emphasizes that Colbert owed his brilliant career to Fouquet's manifold preparations in the areas of finance and economic policy.

ABOVE:
Allegory of Nicolas Fouquet, engraving
by Gilles Rousselet, circa 1660 (detail)

OPPOSITE:
Jean-Baptiste Colbert, painting by
Claude Lefèvre, 1666 (detail)

155

On September 5, 1661 — just three weeks after the fête — Fouquet was arrested. A few days later the Conseil du roi decided to eliminate the superintendency of finance and to create a Conseil royal des finances under the supreme authority of the king. The real winner in the affair was ultimately Jean-Baptiste Colbert, who was named »contrôleur général des finances« in December 1665. From that point on he would gradually take over most of the important political functions.

The trial against Fouquet lasted three years. On December 22, 1664, the tribunal announced its decision and imposed a moderate sentence: exile and confiscation of his property. But Louis XIV proved implacable and ordered lifelong imprisonment. The historian Georges Mongrédien commented, »It is, doubtless, the only example that [French] history offers of the sovereign right of grace exercised for the purpose of increasing the punishment.«[77] On December 27 the last ceremony: accompanied by fifty musketeers Fouquet was brought to Pignerol, a small fortress in the Savoy Alps that served as state prison. He died there in 1680.

It was difficult not to side with Fouquet, but to do so openly required great courage. Jean de La Fontaine — he belonged to the elite group of artists whom Fouquet had supported — possessed such courage. In the hope of mollifying the king, he wrote *Élégie aux nymphes de Vaux*, in which one reads: »Remplissez l'air de cris en vos grottes profondes / Pleurez, Nymphes de Vaux . . .« (Fill the air in your deep grottoes with cries / Weep, o nymphs of Vaux).

As several historians have emphasized, Fouquet's fall marked the end of an epoch in France and the beginning of the Grand Siècle. The fact that the Fouquet affair played out at precisely that time certainly contributed to its tragic proportions: the trial was intended to set an example, and thus the superintendent can be seen as a victim of these new politics. That the king was merely a marionette in Colbert's hands, as is often asserted, is not plausible.

On March 10, 1661, immediately after the death of Cardinal Mazarin, Louis XIV announced to his most important ministers that in the future he would reign alone. And he added: »The stage is changing. In governing my state, in administering my finances, and in negotiating foreign policy, I will follow different principles than those of the late cardinal.«[78] That was six months before Fouquet's fall.

Reflection of the château at Vaux
in the large square pool

It has frequently been emphasized that the king's intention was to use Fouquet to pillory the representatives of an entire generation of royal officials. Jean-Christian Petitfils has written, »To understand the motivations behind this political elimination, a detour by way of Louis XIV's psychology is not unhelpful. In many respects the fall of the house of Fouquet appears to have been like an exorcism of the past pursued by an ardent young man who was concerned with forgetting the omnipresent figure of his mentor.«[79] That is doubtless correct. For further insights into his motives, a look at Louis XIV's *Mémoires* is extremely productive. In the brief passages in which he explains why Fouquet fell into disfavor with him, the latter's passion for art and architecture play an important role: »Seeing the vast establishments that this man had projected, and the insolent acquisitions he had made, could not help but persuade my mind of the excess of his ambition.« And later: »he could not keep himself from continuing his excessive spending, from fortifying certain sites, from decorating his palaces.«[80] The political stage had indeed changed: prior to the era of Louis XIV there was nothing objectionable about a high royal official taking the role of a leading patron of the arts; only now was this seen as a symbol of reprehensible ambition.

LEFT:
Detail from the painting *Le Renommée présente à la France le portrait de Louis XIV* by Jean Nocret, circa 1665

OPPOSITE:
Hand of justice of the French kings, late twelfth or early thirteenth century

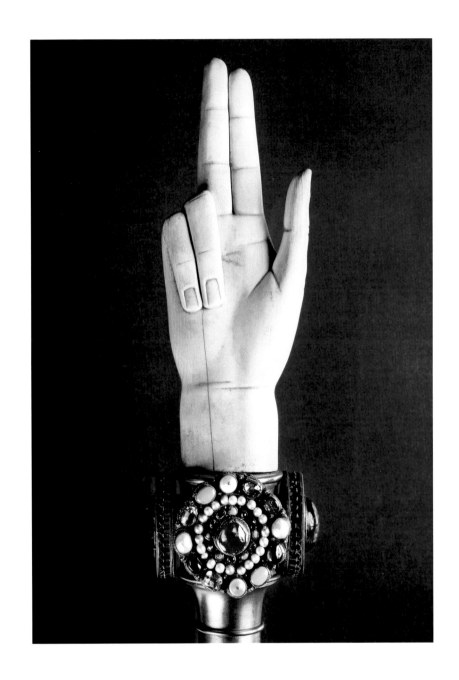

Did Nicolas Fouquet design his château and garden solely with self-interest in mind or did he also consider the glory of the king? In his *Défenses* he claimed that he had decided that Vaux le Vicomte would be the site of his official business and that his prestigious residence would provide evidence of his borrowing power.[81] This statement should not simply be dismissed as a defensive lie, for in the seventeenth century prestige was inconceivable without corresponding external manifestations. The project of Vaux le Vicomte was, moreover, given wing by Fouquet's expectation that he would be Cardinal Mazarin's successor. In that sense, Vaux was supposed to be more than just a private residence: it was, in the words of Marc Fumaroli, »a setting for a Royal Entrance through which Louis XIV would pass to lead France, advised by Foucquet, into an era of plenty and gracious comfort.«[82]

Without a doubt, by realizing his dream the superintendent had given a decisive impulse to the development of the Grand Style. When the king was faced with this total work of art, he recognized its significance for the future. In particular the grandiose effect of the garden gave wing to his own projects for Versailles. In the future he would be the absolute ruler, not only in the field of politics but also in the realm of the arts. He submerged Fouquet's work in darkness so that his own garden would outshine all the others.

ABOVE:
The Grand Degré (large stairway) in the garden at Versailles

OPPOSITE:
View of the northern parterre in the garden at Versailles

Perspective of the garden and park at Versailles

ANDRÉ LE NÔTRE AT VAUX LE VICOMTE

A DOCUMENTATION

CHRONOLOGY: NEW INFORMATION FROM THE EVALUATION OF CONTEMPORARY SOURCES

The history of the site at Vaux le Vicomte is fragmentary and disputed. One set of contemporary documents in particular can help clarify a number of open questions: the archives of Olivier Lefèvre d'Ormesson, which are held in the Archives nationales, Paris. These consist of excerpts from the files that were compiled during the trial against Fouquet and include, among other materials, an extensive report on the expenditures made for Vaux le Vicomte from 1653 on. The report exists in two versions: a rough draft and a fair copy (Fonds d'Ormesson, 144 AP 72, 144 AP 68 / microfilm: 156 MI 27, fols. 38 verso – 46 recto, 156 MI 18, fols. 79 recto – 88 recto). Discrepancies between the two manuscripts frequently provide complementary information. Working from this report and other sources — in particular those published by Jean Cordey in 1924 in his monograph on Vaux le Vicomte — a fairly complete chronology can be established.

This chronology is based primarily on d'Ormesson's report on the construction of Vaux, which is cited extensively and interpreted here for the first time. In order to make the context of the quotations more intelligible, the report's introduction is reproduced here: »Gentlemen of the court — [. . .] the general prosecutor says that the small means that Monsieur Fouquet possessed, the debts he made before His Majesty honored him with the commission of the superintendence, the excessive expenses to which he succumbed since he has been in charge of the king's means, and the effects that remain in his possession after all these excesses — these things are the persuasive proof of the crime of misappropriation of which he is accused« (156 MI 27, fol. 38 verso).

1641
When Nicolas Fouquet acquired the property, his political career was just beginning:
»it should be noted first that he acquired Vaux when he was still master of petitions / That a little while later he made some payments for the construction of a lower court, a parterre, a grove of hornbeams, a kitchen garden, and an orchard; and that all of this was enclosed by walls and consisted of a good forty or fifty acres« (156 MI 18, fol. 79 recto).

1653–1654
In 1653 Nicolas Fouquet was appointed superintendent of finance; he commissioned André Le Nôtre to redesign the existing garden on the basis of a »grander plan.« The first measures were the introduction of water and the canalization of a stream; in addition »the parterre« — that is, the Parterre de la Couronne — was extended (156 MI 18, fol. 79 recto –79 verso; see also p. 24).

1655
The three parterres in front of the château were enlarged and completely redesigned as part of the »grander plan.« In addition, arrangements for the western part of the park were begun (156 MI 18, fol. 79 verso; see also pp. 24–28, including the ills.).

1655–1656
Nicolas Poussin was asked to contribute to the decoration of the garden. Abbé Louis Fouquet, the brother of the superintendent, was to serve as the intermediary in Rome for the commission; the decorations were to include an ensemble of terms, for which Poussin produced clay models. On December 27 the abbé wrote his brother from Rome: »He will make admirable terms for you [. . .],« and in March 1656 he informs him that the completion of the sculptures will require another two months (quoted from Bechter 1993a, 63 and note).

In 1683 Louis-Nicolas Fouquet, the superintendent's son, sold eleven terms to Louis XIV, as indicated in an invoice recorded in the »Comptes des bâtiments du roi«: »To Monsieur le comte DE VAUX for eleven terms of white marble, brought from Vaux to Versailles for the use of His Majesty [. . .]« (quoted from Guiffrey 1887, col. 463). The

Term from the Poussin cycle, detail from the 1728 painting

inventory for Vaux le Vicomte that Jacques Houzeau and Jean Le Grue produced in 1665 makes it possible to identify the eleven terms brought to Versailles and to determine where they stood (the inventory of 1665 is reprinted in Bonnaffé 1882, 69 ff.). They were not, as Sylvain Kerspern supposed, part of an ensemble that would have included the terms of the first parterre zone (1996, 272–73); according to the inventory they were not made of marble at all but had shafts of sandstone and heads »of hard stone« (Bonnaffé 1882, 69; see also ill. on p. 101). Rather, the inventory records »in the large parterre ten half-length terms with arms and attributes, of modern white marble« (Bonnaffé 1882, 70). The term »large parterre« refers to the second parterre, that is, the lawn parterre. The ensemble in the lawn parterre originally included twelve terms, as is clear from the engravings by Perelle and Aveline (*La maison de Vaux le Vicomte . . .*, engraving by Perelle; see ill. on p. 180; *Vue et perspective en general du canal, des grandes cascades et du jardin de Vaux le Vicomte*, engraving by Aveline). The inventory of 1665 records »another term from the same series, still wrapped, in one of the corridors of the château« (Bonnaffé 1882, 70). Clearly this term had been intended as a substitute if one of the others had been damaged during transportation from Rome. Thus the ensemble of eleven terms by Poussin that was sold to Louis XIV was complete. But what happened to the two missing ones, to judge from the twelve terms on the engravings and the ten listed in the inventory?

According to the inventory there were »two additional terms of the same size, half-length figures with arms, of modern white marble, placed to the sides of the Gerbe, above the large cascade [grotto]« (Bonnaffé 1882, 70). Even though these two terms that remained at Vaux le Vicomte may have been assessed at a lower value than the others, they nevertheless belong to the Poussin cycle. They are clearly recognizable in the painting *Visite de la reine Marie Leczynska à Vaux en 1728* (see ill.), where it is evident that even their pedestals share the same type as the terms brought to Versailles (on Poussin's terms, see also Blunt 1966, 148–57; Bechter 1993a, 149–57; Pincas 1996, 169–71).

1656

D'Ormesson's report reads: »in 1656 the house and one side of the moat were begun; [. . .] Gestard, entrepreneur with Courtois, paid the wages at day rates« (156 MI 18, fol. 79 verso). Bénigne Courtois was the intendant of Vaux le Vicomte, while the architect Daniel Gittard (»Gestard«) directed the construction site and carried out the designs of the architect, Louis Le Vau. (ill.: Floor plan of the château, engraving by Rudolf Pfnor.)

By summer, »the foundations of the château walls inside the surrounding walls of the moats and part of the courtyard

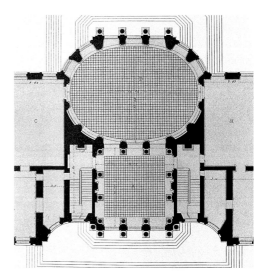

Floor plan of the château (middle section), engraving by Rudolf Pfnor, 1888

were built only to the height of the terraces [...] / Monsieur Fouquet, who perhaps grew tired of this kind of work, in which neither the completion nor the expenditure could be foreseen, wished to continue it with more assurance and understanding « (156 MI 18, fol. 80 recto).

Nicolas Fouquet asked Daniel Gittard to estimate the costs for the construction of the château; this estimate came to »fifteen hundred thirty-one thousand two hundred twenty [i.e., 1,531,220] livres [...]« (156 MI 18, fol. 80 verso). »This calculation proposed to Monsieur Fouquet in 1656, at the beginning of his term as superintendent [*sic*], and in the most difficult times, was such an outlay that neither his personal revenue, nor the earnings from his offices, nor the allocation of the king, who found it difficult to cover his domestic expenses sufficiently, would have been adequate to satisfy it« (156 MI 18, fols. 80 verso − 81 recto). The calculation was presented »to the architect Monsieur LeVeau for review, to indicate the cost savings for each article; by this means the above-mentioned sum of XV.^{C}XXXI.^{M}II.^{C}XX. [i.e., 1,531,220] livres was reduced to VI.^{C}LXIX.^{M}II.^{C}LXX. [i.e., 669,270] livres.« The latter sum is recorded in the dossier; in the fair copy, the sum is, incorrectly, listed as VII.^{C}LXIX.^{M}II.^{C}LXX livres (156 MI 18, fol. 81 recto; 156 MI 27, fol. 41 recto; see also Petitfils, 1998, 179).

»On August 2, 1656, the above-mentioned Monsieur LeVeau, having drawn up an extensive estimate, explained in depth and given in great detail, of all the above-mentioned works that remained to be done for the construction of the new parts of the château of Vaux, consisting of four pavilions, double flights of rooms, and a large oval salon with a vestibule in the center, came to terms with Monsieur Fouquet on the sum of VI.^{C}M [i.e., 600,000] livres for everything; the contract was concluded with their signatures on August 2, 1656 « (156 MI 18, fols. 81 recto − 81 verso). »For the execution of this general contract, the same Monsieur Le Veau made several subcontracts; one with Monsieur de Villedo for the masonry and carpentry«; this subcontract with the entrepreneur Michel Villedo was concluded on August 10, 1656 (156 MI 18, fol. 81 verso). A second subcontract was made with Denis Hébert for the roofing and plumbing.

The two famous designs that show the main facades of the château in outline formed part of these contracts. The design for the facade of the courtyard is signed on the verso by Fouquet, Le Vau, and Villedo, and dated August 2 and 10, 1656. Two months later the project was modified: the masonry of brick and stone that had been planned originally was replaced with masonry consisting entirely of stone (documents reprinted in Cordey 1924, 195, 199). Sandstone from Fontainebleau was selected for the substructure, and sandstone from Creil for the facades.

1657

Other contracts were concluded with Louis Le Vau, »one in 1657 for one side of the outbuildings for a sum of II.^{C}LVII.^{M} [257,000] livres« (156 MI 18, fols. 81 verso − 82 recto). The other side of the outbuildings (*communs*) was entrusted to the architect Antoine Bergeron: »In addition to the contracts above there is another with Monsieur Bergeron alone, for the other side of the outbuildings, for the sum of II.^{C}XXIII.^{M} [223,000] livres« (156 MI 18, fol. 82 recto). The eastern outbuildings were designed by Le Vau; the western ones, by Bergeron.

1656–1657

In coordination with Bénigne Courtois, Daniel Gittard continued the work on the garden, in particular the second parterre zone. After the terrace had been leveled, the square pool and the Allée d'eau could be laid out. The construction for the Grille d'eau was also completed, although it still lacked its decorative sculpture (156 MI 18, fol. 79 verso; see also ill., p. 178). »Certainly it was not possible to locate the details of all the sums that were raised for these expenses; according to the estimates of those familiar with them, the price for them [...] exceeded XI.^{C}M. [11,000] livres« (156 MI 18, fol. 79 verso and 156 MI 27, fol. 40 recto).

1657–1658

»*Plan de Vaux le Vicomte*, an engraving by Israël Silvestre: with this plan (see ill.), the oldest one of the garden and park, Silvestre began his series of engravings documenting the splendors of Vaux. According to d'Ormesson's report Silvestre was working under commission from Nicolas Fouquet; in 1660(?) some of the payments »to Monsieur Silvestre,

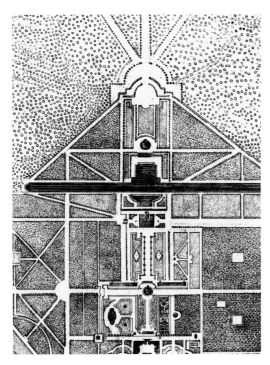

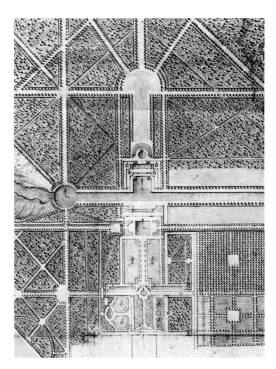

Plan by Israël Silvestre, circa 1657–1658   Plan in the Institut de France, circa 1658–1659

draftsman and engraver« were still owed: »it must be that he is still owed something, as it is noted that Monsieur [Charles] Le Brun is the only one who can judge the works of this Silvestre« (156 MI 18, fol. 84 recto). Silvestre's plan is particularly interesting as it shows a transitional stage in the creation of the garden: the four pools of the lawn parterre have not yet found their final form; the Grand Canal still lacks the large round pool (»la Poële,« literally, the frying pan), which was added later; the large cascade and the grotto are in forms that are considerably simpler than their definitive states; and, finally, the park situated on the far side of the canal is only provisionally sketched in.

1658–1659

A large plan of Vaux le Vicomte, a drawing with watercolor that is bound in a manuscript held in the library of the Institut de France in Paris (Ms 1040, fol. 14): this plan (see ill.), drawn by a collaborator close to André Le Nôtre, is an important document: in contrast to Silvestre's engraved plan, it largely corresponds to the garden and park as they were actually executed, which is reflected in later plans as well, especially the *Parc de Villars* plan (after 1705). It is not a plan in Le Nôtre's own hand, as is often asserted, since the

scrupulously precise style of the drawing clearly deviates from the few surviving sketches that can be attributed with certainty to the gardener (see also ill. on p. 56).

1658–1660

»[In] 1658 Courtois had the large cascade built on day wages, together with the search for the water from Maincy and the aqueducts and the start of work on the canal, the expenses exceeded III.^{C}M [300,000] livres« (156 MI 18, fol. 88 recto).

The architect Antoine Bergeron received payments for the following services: »namely, for the handle of the canal XXX.^{M} [30,000] livres [. . .]. For the two pavilions of the large canal, along with the latter's retaining walls, the large terrace along the Maincy section, fixed at livres XXXVIII.^{M}VI.^{C}IIII.^{XX}V. [38,685] livres« (156 MI 18, fol. 82 verso).

The strange phrase »handle of the canal« is explained by the fact that the Grand Canal, whose eastern end terminates in the large round pool, was called the »frying pan« (»la Poële«). The pavilions are on the western end of the canal. The terrace mentioned is identical with the large allée that runs

The château, detail from an engraving by Israël Silvestre, circa 1659

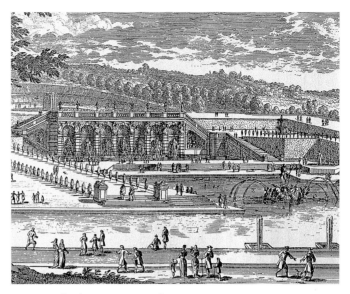

Grotto, Perelle-Silvestre engraving, after 1661

along the western end of the park, or more precisely, between the vegetable garden and the meadow that slopes down to the canal. This allée, which is clearly visible on the plan in the Institut de France (see ill. on p. 56), no longer exists today, although the embankment on which it was built survives.

Gittard continued work on the Grand Canal until 1660. D'Ormesson's report states that Gittard »was paid for the work on the retaining walls of the canal in accordance with the contract that was made with him, covering several articles, from May 8, 1659, to November 17, 1660« (156 MI 18, fol. 83 verso).

1659

»On folio 22 there is mention of a contract for six iron gates for the salon at Vaux, but because Monsieur Hasté the ironworker said that they would cost III.^{M} [3,000] livres each, Monsieur Fouquet reduced the number to just one, for which he was paid II.^{M} [2,000] livres« (156 MI 18, fol. 85 verso). This indication in d'Ormesson's report can help address an unanswered question regarding the garden portals in the Grand Salon. The original plan was probably to provide the arcades with wrought-iron gates only. These arcades correspond with those that connect the salon to the vestibule, as well as with the portals that lead to the main courtyard. When these latter portals — that is, the entrance

arcades — were open, it was possible to see through the entire building into the garden. It is this unique effect that Israël Silvestre reproduces in his engraving (see ill.) and that Madeleine de Scudéry praises in her description of Vaux le Vicomte (see p. 46).

On April 16, 1659, the sculptor Mathieu Lespagnandel concluded a contract with Bénigne Courtois for the sculptural decorations of the Grille d'eau. A memorandum by Lespagnandel, confirmed by Courtois on August 8, 1661, lists the works that had been completed since 1659: »have also made for the small cascade known as *the Grille* ten tables with icicles that are used as pedestals, and have also made twelve masques, namely, six around them and six below, according to the order of my said lord Monsieur [Fouquet]« (document reprinted in Cordey 1924, 225–26, and corresponding note; emphasis in the original). The tasks alluded to are the small fountain basins, made of artificial icicles, and the spouts in the shape of masks (see ills. on p. 178).

1659–1660

A memorandum, on April 16, 1659, by Mathieu Lespagnandel on the sculptures for the grotto and the ramps: »First, two sandstone lions [...] at the start of the two ramps of the said grotto [...] as well as two more that observe them [...]. As well as all the icicles around the two large figures of

Sphinxes by the grotto, detail from the 1728 painting

the rivers [. . .]. As well as one of the said large figures [. . .] depicting the figure of Tiber« (document reprinted in Cordey 1924, 224).

The overall design of the grotto and its sculptures is best documented in the engraving *La grotte de Vaux devant la fontaine de Neptune* by Perelle and Silvestre (see ill.).

Furthermore, the sculptor Blanchard was commissioned to contribute to the decorations of the grotto: »Folio 14 contains the account of Monsieur Blanchard, sculptor, and [it is] indicated that he was paid everything he was owed up to January 14, 1659 / And then an agreement was made with him by Monsieur Le Nôtre for the thirty animals of rocks [. . .], and one of the rivers for VI.^M [6,000] livres« (156 MI 18, fol. 84 verso).

André Le Nôtre concluded an oral agreement with Blanchard for thirty animal figures that were intended as decorations for the artificial rocks in the niches of the grottoes. This ensemble of figures was never executed, however. In his poem *Le songe de Vaux* La Fontaine sketches a scene in which Neptune appears with his Tritons and tells how one of the Tritons advised the sea god to call upon

animals and monsters from many different realms to ornament the grotto: «I will tame them all, and to avoid harm / They will be chained with bronze bonds; / My art will thus decorate these rocks and these niches / For which you reserve the richest treasures« (La Fontaine 1857, 515).

»On folio 31 is the account of Monsieur Lespagnandel, sculptor, according to the contract made with him for II.^M [2,000] for four [lacuna in the manuscript] and six thousand livres for the rivers and the lions, which he received, as well as VI.^C [600] livres extra, all of which totals VIII.^M VI.^C [8,600] livres / And that he should also execute Blanchard's river [god] for XV.^C [1,500] livres. / And that he requested II.^M [2,000] livres for the grille or the ice drops« (156 MI 18, fol. 86 verso). Thus the names of the sculptors who contributed to the decoration of the grotto are indicated, but not the names of the artists who provided the designs for them. The architecture of the grotto, which is so perfectly integrated into the terrain, should be attributed to André Le Nôtre, which is confirmed by the legend of the engraving *La grotte de Vaux devant la fontaine de Neptune* by Perelle and Silvestre: »This grotto owes its design to Monsieur Le Nôtre.« The designs for all the sculptures, however, are by Le Brun, as is evidenced by many indications in the sources.

In addition, these documents also provide information on the history of the grotto's genesis. Mathieu Lespagnandel was commissioned to execute one of the two statues of river gods — namely, Tiber — and the lions that accent the stairs on both sides of the grotto. The other statue of a river god — that of Anqueil — was initially entrusted to the sculptor Blanchard, but in the end it was Lespagnandel who completed it. The four objects that are not named in the manuscript — where a lacuna appears in the corresponding line — were sphinxes. They decorated the ramps that rise next to the grotto and are clearly visible in the painting *Visite de la reine Marie Leczynska à Vaux en 1728* (see ill.). Today the sculptures of the four parts of the earth occupy their places (see ill. on pp. 102–3).

1660–1661
A memorandum by Mathieu Lespagnandel, confirmed by Bénigne Courtois on November 15, 1661: »have also made a

journey to Saint-Leu, at the request of Monsieur Courtois, for the stone for the busts at the grille of the forecourt« (document reprinted in Cordey 1924, 225). Lespagnandel was thus making arrangements for the eight Janus-faced terms of the entrance grille, for which he had selected sandstone from Saint-Leu-d'Esserent in Oise. The designs for these terms were by the sculptor Thibault Poissant. A memorandum by Guillet de Saint-Georges, which dates to the end of the seventeenth century, mentions that Poissant had delivered to Nicolas Fouquet »the stucco models to make eight sandstone terms, each of which is twenty feet high« (La Moureyre and Dumuis 1989, 55, and n. 43). This can only refer to the models for the colossal terms of Vaux le Vicomte, which are indeed about twenty feet high.

A colossal sculpture of Hercules is planned (see ill. on p. 144): »On folio 12 it is indicated that Monsieur Poissant, sculptor, was paid for all his works through the end of 1659. / That he concluded a contract to deliver the plaster model for the large figure of Hercules that he has brought from Rome and to repair something in exchange for III.^{M} [3,000] livres for him and VII.^{M} [7,000] livres for Monsieur Delaporte, beyond which they received two thousand four hundred livres« (156 MI 18, fol. 84 recto). Thibault Poissant was thus supposed to provide a plaster model for the execution of the colossal sculpture, which was probably intended to be cast in bronze. During his sojourn in Rome, Poissant would have had sufficient time to study the famous antique statue in the Palazzo Farnese, with the restorations executed by Giacomo della Porta. When Poissant returned to Paris in 1647, he brought with him a cast of the statue (La Moureyre and Dumuis 1989, 52, and n. 11).

An undated memorandum by the finish carpenter Jacques Prou provides insight into the state of the project at the time of Fouquet's arrest: »Also, I made the model for the pedestal of the large Hercules, including the steps that surround it, according to the order of Monsieur Le Brun« (document reprinted in Cordey 1924, 206).

The garden at Vaux le Vicomte was not completed. Work was disrupted by Fouquet's arrest on September 5, 1661.

In the eighteenth century Vaux le Vicomte came into the possession of the maréchal de Villars, then the duc de Praslin. These changes in ownership resulted in several plans that offer us precise information about the state of the garden at the time.

THE »PARC DE VILLARS« PLAN

In 1705 Nicolas Fouquet's widow sold the château to maréchal Claude Louis Hector de Villars. From 1709 on the domain was designated a ducal peerage and took the name Vaux le Villars. Two plans have survived from the Villars era.

One of these plans, entitled *Parc de Villars*, is undated (see ill.; details, pp. 174, 182). It is bound with a manuscript in the collection of the comte Patrice de Vogüé, the present owner of the château. Several imperfections testify that it was intended as an inventory, not a plan of the ideal state: the embroidery parterre was simplified and planted with grass; the lawn parterre lacks the two pools on the side; finally, the *patte d'oie* (goose foot) behind the present location of the statue of Hercules is incomplete.

THE MAP OF THE DOMAIN OF VILLARS

Under the maréchal de Villars, moreover, a large plan of the entire property was made (see ill. here and on p. 18). This map, which is now located in the stairwell of the château, bears the following legend: »General map of the ducal peerage of Villars and the county of Melun, including the surroundings, around 1754.« The garden and park are reproduced very accurately. Particularly striking is a correction made to the Parterre de la Couronne, relative to its original, asymmetrical state: the southern bed is shortened, which gives the parterre a symmetrical form (on this, see p. 174).

THE PRASLIN A PLAN

In 1764 Honoré Armand, the heir to Claude Louis Hector de Villars, sold the domain to César Gabriel de Choiseul, duc

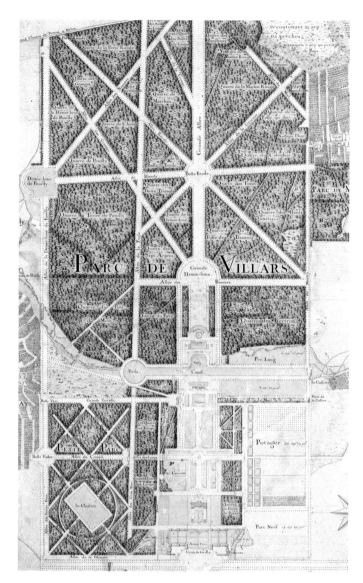

Plan of the garden and park (*Parc de Villars* plan), after 1705

Map of the domains of Vaux-Villars, 1754, detail

Plan of the garden (*Praslin A* plan), after 1764, detail

de Praslin. Two plans of the garden and park have survived from this era. The first extraordinarily large plan, also exhibited in the stairwell of the château, is inscribed »PLAN AND SURVEY OF THE PARC AND CHÂTEAU OF PRASLIN, with the courtyards, the lower courtyards, gardens, parterres, water basins, grottoes, cascades [. . .] contain seven hundred twelve acres [. . .] labeled and numbered according to their state in the years 1735 and 1736« (see ill.). This plan shows the Parterre de la Couronne in simplified form: the three pools that were so characteristic of the original design have disappeared. It also shows that the paths and terraces along the Grand Canal were covered with grass at the time, as can

also be seen in the painting *Visite de la reine Marie Leczynska à Vaux en 1728* (see ill. on p. 170).

THE PRASLIN B PLAN

On this document, which is found in the archives of the department of Seine-et-Marne (»Plan d'intendance de Maincy«: 1 C 50) and may be dated to around 1780 (see ill. on p. 25), the Parterre de la Couronne is shown in a state of complete neglect, but strangely it once again has the asymmetrical form of its original state. The park, with its complex system of allées, appears to be astonishingly well maintained.

RESTORATIONS AND ALTERATIONS IN THE NINETEENTH AND TWENTIETH CENTURIES

The garden at Vaux le Vicomte is, in its present form, the product of a large restoration campaign that took place at the end of the nineteenth and the beginning of the twentieth centuries. This reconstruction, which was based primarily on the engravings by Israël Silvestre, is more or less faithful. Several elements were, however, transformed or left out. In light of the importance that Vaux le Vicomte has for the history of the art of the garden, it seems worthwhile to ascertain the original state and the later deviations as precisely as possible. Such an inquiry can also be helpful in the effort to clarify the question, still disputed today, of Le Nôtre's role in the details of the planning and execution of the garden.

THE FIRST ZONE OF THE GARDEN

From 1653 on the garden was expanded on the basis of Le Nôtre's »grander plan,« which included the new embroidery parterre in a highly extended form. The gardener also lengthened the two lateral parterres — that is, the Parterre de la Couronne and the flower parterre — to create a harmonious ensemble, although it meant these two parterres lost their symmetry (see ill.: detail of the *Parc de Villars* plan; the line marks the extent of the parterre before it was lengthened). In the course of the restoration at the end of the

nineteenth century, the asymmetry was eliminated by shortening the southern beds of both parterres, but this created a new imbalance in the ensemble, as now the two lateral parterres were shorter than the middle one (see ill.: detail of a survey photograph of the garden).

In the case of the old flower parterre, the resulting empty space at the southern end was covered with gravel and bordered by strips of lawn. Later, two sphinxes were placed here, late baroque sculptures from Crisenoy, a nearby château that no longer exists. This change was arranged by duc Théobald de Choiseul-Praslin, who inherited the property in 1841 and began to restore the garden — with the help of his wife, Altatrice Rosalba Fanny — a project that was cut short by his premature death in 1847 (on this, see Moulin 1998, 28).

The embroidery and flower parterres had already lost their original decoration in the eighteenth century, when they were replaced by lawns, as is depicted with great accuracy in the painting *Visite de la reine Marie Leczynska à Vaux en 1728* (see ill.). In the case of the embroidery parterre the extended lawns had rich borders, which can still be seen in the photograph of the neglected garden that was made soon after

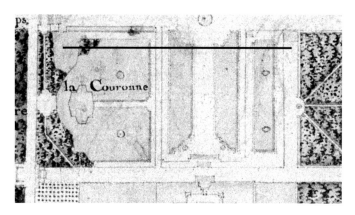

Plan of the garden (*Parc de Villars* plan), after 1705, detail

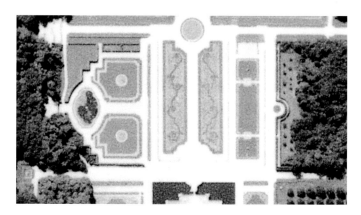

Survey photograph of the garden, detail

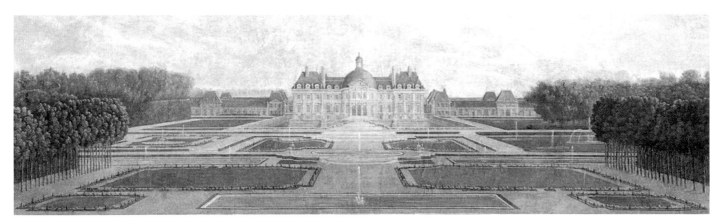

The parterres and the château, detail from the 1728 painting

The parterres and the château, photograph, circa 1875

Vaux le Vicomte was purchased by Alfred Sommier in 1875 (see ill.). The new owner tackled the restoration of the château (Cordey 1924, 177–82), under the direction of the architect Hippolyte Destailleur, who had made his reputation with restorations of châteaus and manors throughout Europe. Destailleur provided much of the initiative for the restoration of the garden, which lay nearly fallow (Cordey 1924, 182–85; Bechter 1993a, 179–88; Bechter 1993b). His collaborator, the gardener Élie Lainé, enriched the lawns of the old flower parterre with boxwood ornaments and established the wide borders of the central parterre (Pfnor 1888, »Plan général en 1887,« see ill. on p. 176).

On Rudolf Pfnor's plan of 1888 the Parterre de la Couronne appears to be a single lawn, and an overgrown one at that.

Alfred Sommier ordered excavations in 1892 to determine the location of the pools. A photograph of the garden taken shortly after 1900 shows the parterre in its restored state (see ill. on p. 176). This restoration was probably undertaken just after 1892 by Henri Duchêne (d. 1902), although his activity at Vaux has been a matter of debate (see Bechter 1993b, 82; Moulin 1998, 28). Duchêne corrected the asymmetry of the parterre that goes back to Le Nôtre by shortening the southern lawn bed (see the ills. on p. 174). He framed the rectangular area that was freed up with a high hedge of yews, and this green space was named the »Table du roi« (King's table). Of the three pools he restored only the one that lies in the axis of the parterre. Finally, he added ornamental borders to the lawns.

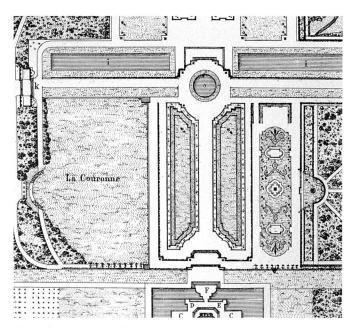

Plan of the garden by Rudolf Pfnor, 1888, detail

Photograph of the garden, shortly after 1900

The activities of Henri Duchêne extended to the two other parterres as well. He enriched the borders of the central parterre, and he altered the ornaments in the lawns of the old flower parterre. The above-mentioned photograph taken shortly after 1900 (see ill.) shows the fruits of the restorations undertaken by Élie Lainé after 1875 and by Henri Duchêne in the 1890s. On the lawns of the central parterre two neobaroque sculpture groups are seen: *L'enlèvement d'Europe* (The abduction of Europe) and *L'enlèvement de Déjanire par Nessus* (The abduction of Dejanira by Nessus). The groups were later removed to the ends of the broad path that runs between the château and the first zone of the parterre.

After the death of Alfred Sommier in 1908 restoration work was continued by his son, Edme Sommier, although it was interrupted again by World War I. Sommier commissioned the landscape architect Achille Duchêne, Henri's son, who began with the parterres on each side of the château (see the aerial photograph on p. 41). There were no documents on which to base this work, since these areas had never had an ambitious design, as the old plans show (see the plan in the Institut de France, ill. on p. 56, and the *Parc de Villars* plan, ill. on p. 172). These two parterres thus represent new creations, and hence are particularly interesting examples of the »style Duchêne.«

Achille Duchêne also made considerable changes to the parterre that had been reworked by his father and Élie Lainé before him. He simplified the ornaments on the lawns of the old flower parterre and reconstructed the two lateral pools of the Parterre de la Couronne, replacing the ornamental borders of the latter with simple strips of lawn. A design for the restoration of the Parterre de la Couronne by Achille Duchêne has survived in the Duchêne estate (illustrated in Bechter 1993a, 133).

Between 1920 and 1923 Achille Duchêne, in close collaboration with Edme Sommier, worked out a definitive conception for the reconstruction of the embroidery parterre, which had been replaced by lawns as early as the eighteenth century. It was modeled on the illustrations by Israël Silvestre (see ill.), although these were interpreted rather freely. Both beds are dominated by a single ornamental path passing through each, consisting of zigzag and curved forms, with the latter frequently curling into tight volutes; tendrils that branch off from these paths constitute a secondary motif (see ill.). Silvestre's drawings and engravings reveal more delicate, less hierarchically articulated ornaments, as well as one particularly beautiful detail that Achille Duchêne did not pick up, namely, the tendrils that extend from the framing of the beds.

Embroidery parterre, detail from an engraving by Israël Silvestre, circa 1658

Embroidery parterre, reconstructed by Achille Duchêne from 1920 onward

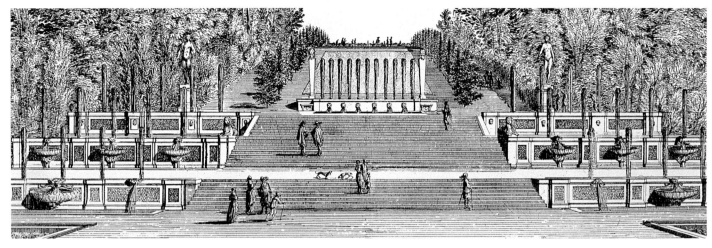

The Grille d'eau, detail from an engraving by Israël Silvestre, circa 1658

The Grille d'eau, present state

The Grille d'eau on the east side of the garden, also known as the »small cascade,« to distinguish it from the »large cascade,« is still part of the first parterre zone. This area was in extremely poor shape already by the middle of the eighteenth century (Dezallier d'Argenville 1972, 243); it was completely renovated beginning in the early 1880s (see ill.). One important element of the original design was ignored, however, namely, the broad fountain found on the terrace above the cascades. Eleven water jets shot up out of this fountain, resembling a crystal grille. The two terms survived, one on each side of the fountain, although they were heavily reworked in the fin-de-siècle style.

As part of this restoration the small cascade was decorated with eighteen stone masks, whereas the original decor had been both more extensive and more varied: twelve grotesque stone masks on the first and second levels of the cascade, and fourteen smaller marble masks on the third level of the cascade and on the broad fountain (report by Mathieu Lespagnandel from August 8, 1661, published in Cordey 1924, 226; inventory by Jacques Houzeau and Jean Le Grue from July 17, 1665, published in Bonnaffé 1882, 70; and the engraving *Vue et perspective des petites cascades de Vaux* by Israël Silvestre, see ill.).

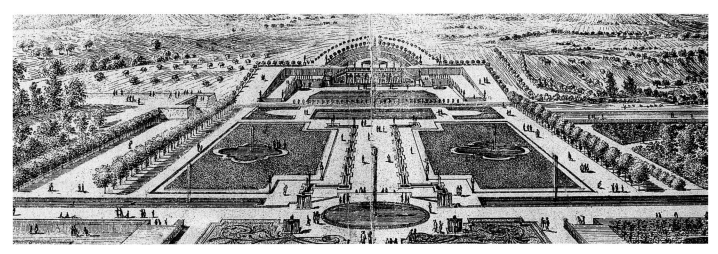

The lawn parterre, detail from an engraving by Israël Silvestre, circa 1658

The lawn parterre, present state

THE SECOND ZONE OF THE GARDEN

The second zone of the garden, the lawn parterre, was also subjected to considerable modifications during the restoration (see ill.: engraving by Israël Silvestre and a photograph of the present state). Today, the parterre is demarcated on the sides by the forest edges with pruned hedges, whereas originally a row of trees was also planted in front of it, and at a considerable distance from it: thus the parterre was lined with allées. This can be seen on all the old plans, as well as in Silvestre's engravings and the painting *Visite de la reine Marie Leczynska à Vaux en 1728* (see the ill. on p. 172). The row of trees was left out, and the two lawn beds were widened to compensate, which gave them too much weight in relation to the embroidery parterre. The two pools in the form of quatrefoils were also enlarged, and their sculptural groups were not at all in harmony with Le Nôtre's original intentions, according to which the pools were planned as simple bodies of water.

The lawn parterre had originally been decorated with the terms executed according to models by Nicolas Poussin, which had been brought to Versailles in 1683 (see ill. on p. 180). Today, this area of the garden is dominated by yews in cone and pyramid shapes. The engravings from Le Nôtre's time already show such pruned trees — along with terms — but they were nowhere near as voluminous as they are today (see ills. on pp. 62–63, 180).

The Allée d'eau and the Poussin terms, detail from an engraving by Perelle, circa 1665

The Allée d'eau, with its vertical jets of water, was originally the main attraction of the second parterre zone, as the engraving *La maison de Vaux le Vicomte* by Perelle clearly reveals (see ill.). Two narrow canals followed the inner contours of the lawn beds, and at regular intervals they expanded to form squares, from each of which a single jet of water shot up. The anonymous chronicler of the fête at Vaux informs us of a peculiarity of these canals, namely that »the water runs between banks with lawns« (»Relation …« 1661, reprinted in Cordey 1924, 192). Similarly, in her description of the Allée d'eau Madeleine de Scudéry uses the eloquent metaphor of »two pretty streams with grassy beds« (Scudéry 1973, 10:1130). When the garden was restored, the canals were replaced by simple strips of lawn and the jets of water by marble bowls (see ill. on pp. 30–31). Today these bowls are planted with flowers.

THE THIRD ZONE OF THE GARDEN: THE CANAL AREA

In the 1880s the two most important structures of the garden, the large cascade and the grotto, were reconstructed under the direction of the architect Hippolyte Destailleur (Garnier 1990; Bechter 1993b).

»The large cascade is completely ruined,« wrote Dezallier d'Argenville (1972, 242). The reconstruction could be based only on several highly deteriorated remnants. The overall layout of twenty individual cascades, separated by pillars, conforms to their state in the seventeenth century (see the ills. on pp. 119–21). Originally each pillar had a grotesque mask from which water spouted into a shell-shaped basin, as can be seen from the painting *Visite de la reine Marie Leczynska à Vaux en 1728* (see ill.). Only two such basins with water spouts were reconstructed, on the outer pillars of the cascade wall.

The large cascade, detail from an engraving by Israël Silvestre, circa 1660

The large cascade, detail from the 1728 painting

In its original state the large cascade offered yet another attraction: a series of twenty-nine jets of water that shot up from the pool.

The upper edge of the cascade, on the level of the terrace, still has twenty-one very small fountains, distributed on the pillars. Originally narrow canals followed the edge of the cascade, and from them twenty more small jets of water shot up. Madeleine de Scudéry wrote that this artifice was made of »very smooth and glistening rock« (1973, 10:1133). These stone canals are also documented in Israël Silvestre's engraving *Vue en perspective des cascades de Vaux* (see ill. on p. 180).

Since the 1880s the two outer pillars of the cascade wall have served as pedestals for groups of marble sculpture, depicting sea horses with playing children, by Alfred Lanson. These

sculptures in the neobaroque style were free additions of the restorers. Both pillars originally had small jets of water, like all the other pillars of the cascade wall.

The grotto was in much better condition than the cascade, although the two river gods by Lespagnandel had to be considerably restored: the statue of Anqueil was largely ruined as an engraving by Rudolf Pfnor shows (1888, »Les grottes [. . .] état en 1883 avant la restauration«), but even the statue of Tiber needed improvement, though it was in a much better state (see ill.). These tasks were entrusted to the sculptor Georges-Louis Hébert.

Of the artificial rocks that fill the niches of the grotto, at least three look as if they might be the heads of monsters (see pp. 130–31 and the illustrations). They can also be seen on Silvestre's engraving *Vue et perspective de la grotte et d'une partie*

The grotto with the statue of Anqueil, engraving by Rudolf Pfnor, 1888

The statue of Tiber at the grotto, engraving by Rudolf Pfnor, 1888

Rock fountains of the grotto, detail from an engraving
by Israël Silvestre, circa 1660

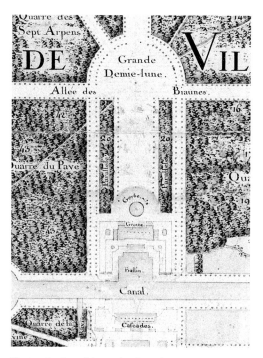

The termination of the garden from the
Parc de Villars plan, after 1705

du canal (see ill.). In his brief description of the garden at Vaux, Antoine-Joseph Dezallier d'Argenville mentions »seven rocky niches, with animals that shoot out water« (1972, 243). Even if these monsters are in a rather ruined state today, they can still be recognized. The animal in the niche at far right, however, is a more recent addition.

In the early 1880s the ramps on both sides of the grotto were decorated with a group of four marble sculpture groups depicting the four parts of the earth (then known to baroque Europe), works by the sculptor Émile Peynot (see the ills. on pp. 102–3). Although they were planned but never executed in her day, these groups were inspired by Madeleine de Scudéry's description, which mentions sculptures on this theme. Contemporaneous engravings and the painting *Visite de la reine Marie Leczynska à Vaux en 1728* (see the ill. on p. 170) show sphinxes where the *Quatre parties du monde* by Peynot now stand.

THE PARK BEYOND THE GARDEN

The semicircular plaza located above the grotto is so far away that it really belongs more to the park than to the garden. In 1891 the gigantic statue of Hercules, about twenty-one feet

high, was placed here (see the illustrations on pp. 139, 146). This sculpture, based on a model by Joseph Tournois, was cast in lead and gilt by the firm Thiébaut Frères (see Garnier 1990, 77). The backdrop of trees that lines the side of the slope is greatly simplified in comparison to the original state, which is documented on the plan in the Institut de France as well as the *Parc de Villars* plan and is still recognizable on later plans: the lateral allées that continue those of the lawn parterre are now lacking. These allées began at the ramps of the grotto and came together to form a semicircle at the very top. Rows of densely planted trees were placed along the allées, and in front of that, at a distance equal to the width of the allée, another row of trees was planted (illustrations: detail from the *Parc de Villars* plan and detail of the survey photograph of the garden).

CONCLUSION

The restoration of the garden was carried out at a time very favorable to such a project: namely, in the last phase of historicism. That era developed a lively interest in the varied styles of the past, and the art of the baroque in particular was rediscovered. It was this stimulating context that led the German architect Rudolf Pfnor to publish his album of

The termination of the garden, detail from a survey photograph

The terraces of the garden and the château, engraving by Rudolf Pfnor, 1888

engravings of the château at Vaux, a work of remarkable quality that focused primarily on architecture (Pfnor 1888; see ill.).

The extensive campaign to restore the garden at Vaux that had been begun by the industrialist Alfred Sommier in 1875 was a decisive contribution to the rediscovery of Le Nôtre's style: »One can compare, symbolically, the taste for geometric gardens and the 'restoration' of the château and park at Vaux le Vicomte« (Mosser 2000, 49–50). The

Sommier family, father and son, was increasingly concerned, during the various phases of reconstruction, with historical fidelity. In this respect the successive restorations of the parterres in front of the château represent an instructive example, even though the end results have significant deviations from the original state. Similar modifications were made by the restorers in other parts of the garden as well. Even so, it is fair to say that its appearance today offers a largely reliable picture of Le Nôtre's first great masterpiece.

GLOSSARY

Allée d'eau

An extended structure consisting of two rows of water jets that shoot up to form an »avenue« of water. In the Allée d'eau that Le Nôtre designed for Vaux, which has not survived, the water rose out of small, grass-banked canals and drained into them as well. The Allée des Marmousets at Versailles followed the model of the Allée d'eau at Vaux; according to a contemporaneous report it was executed based on an idea by Claude Perrault. Here at Versailles the lawns have rows of fountains from which the water jets rise.
See illustrations on pages 117, 180

Anamorphosis

An anamorphic image is one in which a figure, an object, or a landscape is depicted in extreme distortion, either compressed or extended, so that an enigmatic image results. Only when viewed from an extremely narrow acute angle, or with the help of a conically or cylindrically shaped mirror, does an image result that corresponds to the reality of our experience. The most famous example is the shield with the skull on Hans Holbein the Younger's painting *The Ambassadors.* Such curiosities of perspective were a frequently discussed theme in Le Nôtre's day, and the master of the art of gardening was probably inspired by them. According to a note by Marguerite Charageat (1955, 71) this suspicion had already been expressed by the landscape architect Achille Duchêne, who established a connection between the design of the parterres at Vaux and anamorphic images. If the garden at Vaux is compared to gardens from the sixteenth or early seventeenth centuries, its outline seems distorted — specifically, increasingly expanded the further its parts are from the viewer. As perceived optically, however, the parterres and their pools present harmonic proportions: the distortion disappears as a result of the extremely acute angle of view with which it is observed. When Achille Duchêne reconstructed the embroidery parterres in the 1920s he rigorously followed the method that Le Nôtre had once practiced. In aerial views the tendril ornaments seem deformed, as if stretched out along their length; in normal perspective they appear compressed, in a quasi-baroque fullness.
See illustrations on pages 87, 89-91, 174 (right)

Atlantes

Atlantes are larger-than-life male figures used to support the entablature of an architectonic structure. They can also consist of simple pillars below, with only the upper part forming a figure. Such atlantes decorate the grotto at Vaux, which was designed by André Le Nôtre and Charles Le Brun working in collaboration.
See illustrations on pages 109, 128, 129

Bosquet

An area separated from the forest by walls consisting of hedges and/or trellises. This space under the open sky is usually decorated by artificial arrangements of water. A bosquet can be designed as a labyrinth or a structure of allées and plazas based on a geometric plan. All of these variations were once represented at Versailles. The Salle de Bal bosquet, designed by Le Nôtre, has survived. In recent years there have been extensive efforts at Versailles to reconstruct the bosquets that did not survive. The first, highly persuasive outcome of these efforts was revealed to the public in 1997: the reconstructed Bosquet de l'Encelade. It is an exemplary demonstration of the playful baroque style that Le Nôtre preferred when designing these intimate spaces, in contrast to the strict classical style that he used when designing the large, open spaces of the garden. Prior to Versailles, Le Nôtre had designed two bosquets for Vaux. The Cloître (cloister) in the eastern section of the park was gigantic. It consisted of a system of allées and plazas, much like a labyrinth. Traces of the Cloître can still be seen clearly in aerial photographs. A second bosquet was found in the section of the park that borders on the village of Maincy. It was an open-air hall with an exedra; in the center it had a *montagne d'eau,* an artificial crag with waterfalls.
See illustrations on pages 19, 56, 123

Cascade

An artificial waterfall in a sloping part of the terrain. It is an essential element in Italian gardens of the Renaissance and baroque. Water staircases were particularly popular, such as those of the Villa Lante in Bagnaia, the Villa Farnese in Caprarola, and the Villa Aldobrandini in Frascati. Bernini designed the cascade beneath the water organ at Tivoli as a wild mountain slope with artificial crags and roaring waterfalls (no longer extant). Le Nôtre designed numerous cascades. In the Salle de Bal bosquet at Versailles there is a stepped cascade integrated into an oval amphitheater. Its design is decidedly rustic. By contrast, the water staircase at Sceaux,

Garden of Vaux le Vicomte: Longitudinal section

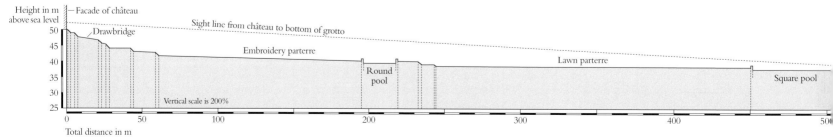

which was reconstructed in a simplified form around 1930, reveals monumental and strict forms. Le Nôtre chose for Vaux a wall cascade — a wall with spouting masks and fountain bowls arranged in several stories. The Cascade Gondi at Chantilly, also designed by Le Nôtre, falls into this same category.
See illustrations on pages 82, 118–123

Embroidery Parterre
The most noble part of a French garden, placed directly in front of the château. It is decorated with complicated ornaments — arabesques or tendrils — in the style of embroidery. The main lines of the ornaments consist of cut boxwood; the fill consists of small patches of grass and bright sand, frequently in alternation with crushed coal. These are supplemented — sparsely — by low-growing flowers or ornamental bushes. The embroideries at Vaux are a reconstruction from the 1920s with the ornaments simplified and red brick chippings in lieu of sand. In its present state the Parterre du Midi in Versailles gives an approximate idea of the original embroideries, although the proportion of flowers is too high. Le Nôtre originally designed the middle parterre at Versailles with embroideries very similar to those at Vaux, but it was later replaced by the existing water parterre (see »Water Parterre«).
See illustrations on pages 26–27, 34–35, 66–69, 73, 177

Étoile
In the art of gardening an *étoile* is a circular plaza with trees pruned to form walls of greenery and allées radiating out in a star-shaped pattern. Le Nôtre employed such an *étoile* at Vaux, and it became the focus of the park's vast system of allées; it has survived only in rudimentary form. The greatest example is the Étoile Royale at the end of the central axis at Versailles, which is currently being reconstructed. The *étoiles* in Le Nôtre's gardens became the models for similar plazas in the great cites of the eighteenth and nineteenth centuries: Berlin, Washington, and Paris.
See illustrations on pages 25, 172

Fabriques (Staffage Buildings)
Small buildings used as picturesque accents in a garden. They are designed to be pluralistic in style and are intended to evoke the cultures of other eras and lands. *Fabriques* are typical of the English garden as it evolved from the middle of the eighteenth century onward. There is evidence of an unusually early example at Vaux, if only of a stage of a project that could not be realized, owing to Fouquet's arrest. It consisted of two pyramids that were supposed to include various antique curiosities from Fouquet's collection, in particular two Egyptian sarcophagi that later entered the collections of the Louvre. The project, proposed by Charles Le Brun, was described in detail by Madeleine de Scudéry as if it had actually been realized. The pyramids were supposed to be constructed on the western side of the garden, near the large square pool, or more precisely where the »grande allée en terrasse« leads into the garden. The meadow that descends from this terrace down to the Grand Canal was to be cultivated as a vineyard, and there were also plans for »plusieurs objets champêtres« — that is to say, more *fabriques*, which in this case were supposed to evoke an idyllic rural life.

Flower Parterre
According to the rules of the French garden, the flower parterre was never in the central axis: »The flower garden must be to one side and calls for sandy and airy soil« (Mollet 1981, 25). One exception is the legendary parterre of the secondary château at Versailles, the Grand Trianon, which was immediately in front of the château. It was densely planted with flowers, some of which were very fragrant: tulips, hyacinths, narcissi, wallflowers, violets, and tuberoses. At Vaux the flower parterre is on the western side of the garden. There the flowers and ornamental bushes were once planted so as to form artful ornaments, like embroideries but even more delicate. No trace of this can be found in the present planting, which consists of large surfaces, but there are plans to reconstruct this parterre in a way closer to its original state.
See illustrations on pages 70–72

French Garden
The French garden was the representative garden genre of the baroque age, and it was adopted throughout Europe. Several of its principles evolved even before Le Nôtre's day, but he was the artist who perfected them and brought them into a coherent system. The French garden differs from the Renaissance in having greater dimensions and a clear spatial unity. The central axis is dominant: it is unobstructed and often extends to the horizon, as it does at Vaux, Versailles, and Meudon. The subdivision by means of elemental geometric forms like the square and circle that were common in the Renaissance garden is replaced by a composition based on larger and more complex forms that can produce the effects of *perspective ralentie* (see »Perspective Ralentie«). The genre of the quasi-natural English garden caught on beginning in the middle of the eighteenth century. The French garden began to be sharply criticized, for example by Marc-Antoine Laugier, who wrote of Versailles in his *Essai*

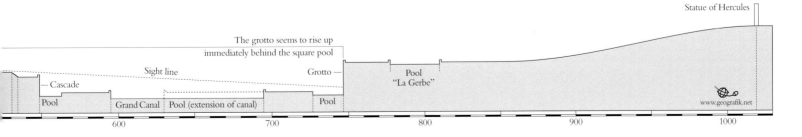

sur l'architecture, published in 1755, that there nature was »entombed, buried under an extravagant apparatus of symmetry and magnificence.« In England in particular the polemic against the French garden was associated with a fundamental critique of absolutism.

Grand Canal

The dimensions of the canals that Le Nôtre built in his gardens are enormous: the length of the canal at Vaux is more than half a mile long; at Sceaux, three-quarters of a mile; at Versailles, a mile; and at Chantilly, a mile and a half. Fed by small rivers these controlled bodies of water are an especially impressive demonstration of this gardener's art of ennobling nature and lending it grandiose forms. The Grand Canal extends the space of the garden into infinity; at Versailles this ribbon of water, which continues the central axis of the garden, reaches the horizon. Le Nôtre's proud description of how he had miraculously transformed a river into a canal »without end« is particularly revealing; he adds, significantly, that one should not inquire about the origin of the water, because — his subordinate clause seems to suggest — it remains the artist's secret (see Le Nôtre to the Earl of Portland, July 11, 1698, on p. 100 of this volume). The relationship between the large canals in Le Nôtre's gardens and the shipping canals that were being built in France at that time is obvious. At the court of the Sun King there were discussions of a project to build a canal that would lead from the Loire to Versailles. Le Nôtre responded enthusiastically, »what a pleasing thing it would be to see the vessels descending [from] the river Loire with their masts and sails along the mountain [of Satory, near Versailles], like a glissade, and to come floating down the grand canal« (Charles Perrault, *Mémoires*, quoted in Mariage 1999, 87).
See illustrations on pages 102-3, 116, 143

Grotto

The most beautiful effects of a garden are due to water: pools in which distant buildings are reflected, allées seemingly of crystal, and canals of enormous dimensions. The grotto is the place where the mythical origins of this element are made visible. It is a rustically designed cave; the most famous example is Buontalenti's Grotta Grande in the Boboli Gardens. Such caverns offered an opportunity to install automatons and water organs. The grottos of Saint-Germain-en-Laye (around 1600, no longer extant) were rich in such curiosities. For Jacques Boyceau (1638, 80) such features are still obligatory in grottos: they »are created to represent the animal dens [. . .]. They are ornamented with rustic works [. . .]. The water can also be used to drive engines and machines [. . .].« Ándre Le Nôtre did not hold to these conventions. He designed the grottos as forceful walls with niches. The grotto at Vaux, which he designed together with Charles Le Brun, is a masterpiece. The grotesque aspect of the genre is merely suggested in stylized forms — for example, in a series of rock fountains — and it is integrated into a strict facade with a classical feeling. The grotto at Chantilly is less monumental; it was primarily designed by Jules Hardouin-Mansart; Le Nôtre probably added only the niches with river gods. The once famous Thetis grotto at Versailles, designed by the Perrault brothers, picked up on the tradition of caverns but in the garden of the Sun King this genre was reinterpreted as a magnificent vaulted hall, fitted out with noble marble sculptures that are now located in the bosquet of the Bains d'Apollon.
See illustrations on pages 109, 110, 124-131

Jardinier (Garden Artist)

The gardens of the Italian Renaissance were designed by architects: Vignola, Tribolo, and Ligorio. In France, from the late sixteenth century onward, this task was taken by professional gardeners. Some of them were educated and able to write treatises: Claude I Mollet (1610s, published posthumously in 1652), Jacques Boyceau (1638), and André Mollet (1651). The themes of these treatises ranged widely: from theory of climate by way of agriculture on to natural philosophy. Questions of artistic design were not primary, but they already occupied a considerable portion of the works of Jacques Boyceau and Claude Mollet. Le Nôtre is the towering figure in this »dynasty« of professional gardeners and in due course significantly elevated this métier to the rank of an art. There is no treatise by him, however, not even any remarks on the theory of gardening. He was a man of the building site. Le Nôtre's genius, praised by his contemporaries, cannot be appreciated from any theories or remarks but only from his surviving gardens or from his plans.

Kitchen Garden

In the Renaissance era the ornamental kitchen garden was integrated into the ensemble of the princely garden. The planting of vegetables followed artful, delicate ornaments. The famous garden of Villandry gives a sense of this; it was reconstructed in the early twentieth century on the basis of engravings by Jacques Androuet du Cerceau. Le Nôtre resolutely excluded the kitchen garden from the large perspectives of his landscapes, which are conceived as pure art. At Saint-Mandé, the garden for which is documented in a beautiful plan that can be attributed to Le Nôtre, the kitchen garden was enclosed by walls. Although that kitchen garden was ornately designed, the one at Vaux was divided very simply, solely on the basis of utility, as is clear from the plan in the Institute de France.
See illustrations on pages 44, 56, 78, 79

Lawn Parterre

The lawn parterre is nearly always subordinated to or juxtaposed with the main parterre that extends out in front of the château: »The lawn parterres or beds are placed behind the embroidery parterres« (Mollet 1981, 31). These beds have a pool at the center, or sometimes a group of pools — as is the case at Chantilly, where the lawn parterres are extraordinarily large and represent, also unusually, the garden's dominant ornament. During the reconstruction in the nineteenth century the old borders of ornamental bushes, flowers, and small pruned trees were abandoned, with the result that the areas of lawn and water seem

even more generous and modern than in their original state. One popular subgenre of the lawn parterre in the seventeenth century was the *parterre de gazon coupé* (cutout lawn parterre), in which the lawns were subdivided by paths of brightly colored sand to produce spacious arabesques or palmettes. The parterre of the Orangerie at Versailles, reconstructed in 2001, is an impressive example of this. A similar reconstruction of the Parterre de Latone in the same garden is under way. Both these *parterres de gazon coupé* were designed by Le Nôtre. The lawn parterre at Vaux was designed by Le Nôtre without any borders or other ornaments.
See illustrations on pages 29, 33, 34–35, 75, 179

Modeling of the Terrain
In his gardens Le Nôtre achieved startling effects of optical illusions by manipulating the natural terrain: aggradations, terracing, and clefts in the form of wide trenches. In calculating the planes and their levels he made use of the advances that had been made in surveying during the seventeenth century, borrowing methods that had been tried and tested in the construction of fortresses. The compositions of ramps and terraces at both Vaux and Versailles recall such works of military architecture. One of the most important achievements in fortification was, as Thierry Mariage has shown, the »projet irrégulier« that Le Nôtre transferred to his garden: he used the irregularities of the terrain, even increased them, and in this way achieved his unparalleled spatial effects. Vaux, Versailles, and Chantilly offer sufficient illustration. Le Nôtre's boldest »projet irrégulier« is the park at Sceaux, with its dizzying perspectives that result from the enormous leaps in the elevation of the terrain. Le Nôtre always had the sometimes descending, sometimes ascending parts of the terrain arranged so that the viewer could gaze over them in the optimal way. The descending areas are terraced so that the viewer can see even the most distant terraces from above, to some degree — this is the case at Vaux and Sceaux. The ascending parts, in the distant part of the garden, are designed as lawns sloping toward the viewer. Examples may be found

at Vaux, Chantilly, and Saint-Cloud. Where the terrain had extended horizontal spaces, Le Nôtre organized them so that in perspective they seem highly compressed; the clearest example is the plane at Versailles that contains the Grand Canal.
See illustrations on pages 82, 98–99, 106, 107, 112, 143

Miroir d'eau (Water Mirror)
A pool in which a building is entirely reflected, even though it stands at a great distance. Le Nôtre is the inventor of this optical trick, and visitors to Vaux encounter it twice: in the large square pool of the lawn parterre and in the oval pool of the Parterre de la Couronne. In both cases the surprising effect is that the distant château and its reflection, which is quite close to the eye, have almost equal presence. Le Nôtre created another *miroir d'eau* in the park at Sceaux: the pool of the Terrasse des Pintades. In all three cases the effect of the mirror results from the terracing of the garden: the level on which the château is located is substantially higher than that of the water's surface (see »Modeling of the Terrain«). These beautiful reflections occur only exceptionally, however, since Le Nôtre conceived his gardens to be so spacious and open that a lull in the wind is extremely rare.
See illustrations on pages 77, 85, 96–97, 157

Patte d'oie (Goose Foot)
A semicircular plaza from which several (usually three) paths or allées radiate. There were four *pattes d'oie* at Vaux: two on the western side of the garden and one each in front of the château and the park, in the latter case behind where the statue of Hercules is now located. A monumental version of the *patte d'oie* is found in the three avenues that extend far into the town and country from the Place d'Armes in front of the château at Versailles; without a doubt it was designed by Le Nôtre. This pattern for a structuring of space that is as clear as it is complex — related to a center and yet expansively reaching out — already had its followers in the baroque period; the most famous example is the ideal plan for the princely residence in Karlsruhe (1715).

There the *patte d'oie* is integrated into the figure of an *étoile* of gigantic dimensions (see »Étoile«).
See illustrations on pages 56, 57, 172

Perspective
The means by which objects existing in space are depicted on a plane, in a way analogous to optical perception. For such planar projections Renaissance artists developed scientifically based methods: linear perspective, based on Euclidian geometry, and aerial perspective. Their goal was to depict the objects in space so that their relationships — width, height, depth — seemed to be objectively correct, that is, seemed to correspond to experiential reality. These relationships had a harmonic effect only when the spaces involved were extended moderately. Because perspective was thought to coincide with vision, it was thought to be reliable. In the seventeenth century, particularly in France, the theoretical opinion began to take hold that perspective — and, more generally, optical perception — was not reliable but rather a source of misjudgments, even illusions (Descartes, Niceron). The theory of the art of gardening was not unaffected by this; in particular, the unsightly distorting effects of perspective became a theme. Jacques Boyceau described them as an error of vision — »le defaut de la veuë« (1638, 72); André Mollet gave precise advice on how a gardener could correct this error (1651, 31). Drastic corrective measures are required when the garden extends toward the horizon over distances of more than half a mile (Vaux) to nearly two miles (Versailles). Le Nôtre braved the challenge and applied a method in designing these gardens that we might call, hyperbolically, reversed perspective (see »Perspective Ralentie«).
See illustrations on pages 29, 94–95

Perspective Ralentie (Decelerated Perspective)
Perspective ralentie counteracts the fact that the eye's perception of a space and the objects located within it is based on an acute perspectival distortion whereby distant objects appear infinitesimal. Le Nôtre corrects for this »error of vision« by

designing the various parts of the garden to be progressively larger as they become more distant. This is a radical break from the design principles of the Renaissance garden, which was structured according to modules and hence according to the same scale relationships throughout. The startling effects of *perspective ralentie* are found in the garden at Vaux: there are enormous size differences between the embroidery parterre and the lawn parterre, as well as between the pools of those parterres. Other examples include the two pools on the main axis of the garden of the Tuileries in Paris and the three pools of the Grand Canal at Versailles.

See illustrations on pages 29, 32

Plants and Trees
Flowers are extremely rare in Le Nôtre's gardens (see »Embroidery Parterre« and »Flower Parterre«). A more important role is played by evergreen yews, pruned into conical or pyramidal shapes. They are abundantly represented at Vaux and Versailles; there are gigantic examples still standing at Sceaux and Saint-Cloud, but they are not in Le Nôtre's style. Decoratively shaped boxwood trees were especially popular, clipped into bizarre shapes that recall decorative vases and table ornaments. They were borrowed from Italian Renaissance gardens and have their origin in the *ars topiaria* as practiced in the gardens of Roman antiquity (see »Topiary«). At Versailles many of these bizarre creatures of the art of the garden are present again in recent years: in the Allée d'eau, in the Parterre de Latone, and in the Allée royale. The large perspectives of Le Nôtre's gardens are characterized by green walls of hornbeam, elm, and maple, as can be seen at Sceaux and Versailles, thanks to recent restorations, although elms are no longer found, as they are practically extinct in Europe. These green walls, reaching heights of thirty feet, outline the forests and accompany the allées. The forest was the greatest investment in a French garden. At Vaux the reforestation of the barren terrain preceded the layout of the garden. Louis XIV had full-grown trees brought to Versailles on carts from distant royal woods.

See illustrations on pages 62-63, 82, 117, 143, 144

Renaissance Gardens
The Italian garden of the Renaissance was associated with a villa, as in Tivoli (Villa d'Este), Florence (Villa Medicea di Castello), and Bagnaia (Villa Lante). It is structured by means of elemental geometric forms: rectangles, squares, circles, and so on. Large gardens are subdivided into autonomous areas. There is a continuous central axis along which vertical accents are placed: extravagant fountains or groves of trees in geometrical forms. The French garden of the Renaissance is associated with a château. Its division into elemental geometric forms follows the Italian model. The garden is always enclosed by walls or extended buildings that open up onto galleries. Artful fountains are indispensable, usually with a pavilion built above them. These structures create powerful vertical accents. Where the terrain permits, the garden is terraced. The hanging gardens of Saint-Germain-en-Laye, built from 1594 onward for Henry IV, were famous. There the retaining walls of the terraces opened up onto grottos decorated with automatons and other curiosities. None of the French gardens of the Renaissance have survived, but many were documented in Jacques Androuet du Cerceau's *Les plus excellents bâtiments de France*, published in 1576 and 1579.

See illustrations on pages 92, 93

Term
A pillar that tapers toward the base and whose upper portion consists of a bust or half-length figure depicting a divinity or other mythological being; a simpler variant is a pillar with only a head on it. Terms were borrowed from antiquity and became a popular item in Italian Renaissance gardens and later in baroque gardens. At Vaux they were both numerous and varied in form. The cycle of terms designed by Nicolas Poussin that once stood in the lawn parterre was later brought to Versailles. Colossal terms with two-sided busts decorate the grill at the entrance to the forecourt of the château at Vaux. Terms

of the simpler type, with heads only, are placed along the edges of the flower parterre and the Parterre de la Couronne at Vaux as well. During the long construction period for the garden at Versailles terms were increasingly replaced by more ambitious, full-length sculptures.

See illustrations on pages 47-53, 101, 166, 178, 180

Topiary
The art of pruning trees or bushes in decorative geometric or figurative forms was practiced in Roman antiquity. This *ars topiaria* enjoyed a revival in the gardens of the Renaissance. In the French gardens of the baroque such bizarre forms, usually of pruned boxwood, were still well represented. In recent years they have been meticulously reconstructed at Versailles (see »Plants and Trees«). At first glance, these extravagant artworks in miniature seem alien within the context of the classical forms that Le Nôtre used to organize the space of his gardens, but this reveals a typical feature of baroque art: the penchant for contrast between large and small forms.

See illustration on page 117

Water Parterre
A main parterre in which the traditional embroidery beds have been replaced by pools. Le Nôtre originally designed the middle parterre at Versailles with embroideries, as decreed by tradition. Around 1670 they were removed in favor of a bombastic project by Charles Le Brun: a five-part ensemble of pools, ornamented by a host of marble statues. This structure was begun but then removed and, beginning in 1683, replaced by the existing water parterre, which is distinguished by its large and startlingly simple forms. The design is usually attributed to Jules Hardouin-Mansart, but it may be assumed that Le Nôtre played a significant role in the planning. Le Nôtre (or the architect Girard) designed a water parterre for Saint-Cloud that consisted of a single large, sinuously curved pool, the Bassin des Cygnes. It extends under the château's terrace and is enclosed by curving ramps.

See illustrations on pages 64-65

NOTES

SOURCES FOR THE EPIGRAPHS

p. 8   JEAN-BAPTISTE COLBERT, quoted from Chéruel, 1862, 2:545

p. 20 ARCHIVES D'OLIVIER LEFÈVRE D'ORMESSON, 156 MI 18, fol. 79 recto

p. 36 PÈRE DESMOLETS, 1726, quoted from Mariage, 1999, 98
       INSCRIPTION on Le Nôtre's tomb memorial in the church of Saint-Roch, Paris, illustrated in Keller-Dorian, 1920, pls. 104, 106

p. 46 SCUDÉRY, 1973, 10:1100–1102

p. 60 SCUDÉRY, 1973, 10:1092–1093
       SCUDÉRY , 1973, 10:1132

p. 84 DESCARTES, 1972, 66–68
       CHANTELOU, 1663, 11, 13–14

p. 100 SCUDÉRY, 1973, 10:1132.
       ANDRÉ LE NÔTRE to the Earl of Portland, July 11, 1698, quoted from Garnier-Pelle, 2000, 13
       ACHILLE DUCHÊNE, correspondence, quoted in Frange 1998, 36

p. 114 LA FONTAINE, 1857, 515, 506
       ARCHIVES D'OLIVIER LEFÈVRE D'ORMESSON, 156 MI 18, fol. 84 verso

p. 136 ARCHIVES D'OLIVIER LEFÈVRE D'ORMESSON, 156 MI 18, fol. 84 recto
       UPDATED REPORT BY JACQUES PROU, carpenter, published in Cordey, 1924, 206
       INVENTORY OF VAUX, September 1661, published in Bonnaffé, 1882, 90–91

p. 148 ANONYMOUS, »Relation des magnificences faites par Monsieur Fouquet à Vaux-le-Vicomte…,« reprinted in Cordey, 1924, 193
       MOTTEVILLE, 1723, 225–226

NOTES TO PAGES 10 TO 160

1   MORAND, 1961, 15.
2   MARIAGE, 1990, 97.
3   FOUQUET, 1696, 9:124.
4   Most authors including Aurélia Rostaing in a recent study, mention the year 1655; others, including Franklin Hamilton Hazlehurst and Nicole Garnier-Pelle, are even inclined to date it to 1656.
5   See PÉROUSE DE MONTCLOS, 1997, 101, 204n4.
6   DEZALLIER D'ARGENVILLE, 1972, 242.
7   WEBER, 1985, 90.
8   LUCAS, 1988, 129–34.
9   PETITFILS, 1998, 188.
10 JESTAZ, 1991, 17–19.
11 DEZALLIER D'ARGENVILLE, 1972, 97.
12 KELLER-DORIAN, 1920, pls. 104, 106.
13 CAUMONT, 2000, 91.
14 WEBER, 1985, 91.
15 This plan is held by the Nationalmuseum, Stockholm.
16 DEZALLIER D'ARGENVILLE, 1972, 242.
17 WOODBRIDGE, 1986, 184.
18 PFNOR, 1888, 70.
19 See BRATTIG, 1998, 243n715.
20 HAZLEHURST, 1980, 24–28.
21 SCUDÉRY, 1973, 10:1102.
22 MARIAGE, 1999, 104; 1990, 125.
23 SAINT-SIMON, 1985, 532.
24 Quoted from GARNIER-PELLE, 2000, 8–9.
25 See ROSTAING, 2000, 17n9.
26 MOLLET, 1981, 33.
27 Ibid., 33, 35; BOYCEAU, 1638, 73.
28 BOYCEAU, 1638, 73; MOLLET, 1981, 33.
29 BOYCEAU, 1638, 30, 68, 69.
30 MOLLET, 1981, 34.
31 SAINT-SIMON, 1983, 739.
32 CORPECHOT, 1912, title.
33 WOODBRIDGE, 1986, 71–72.
34 DEZALLIER D'ARGENVILLE, 1712, 3; DEZALLIER D'ARGENVILLE, 1709, 3.
35 BOYCEAU, 1638, 69.
36 Ibid., 72.
37 Ibid., 75.
38 Ibid., 30.
39 MOLLET, 1981, 31.
40 Ibid., pls. 2, 5, 12.
41 CHARAGEAT, 1954, 68, 71.
42 See BALTRUŠAITIS, 1984, 49; BALTRUŠAITIS, 1977, 50.
43 NICERON, 1638 and Niceron, 1646.
44 See BALTRUŠAITIS, 1984, 49, 51; BALTRUŠAITIS, 1977, 50.
45 WEISS, 1995, 33 (subtitle).
46 See AURICOSTE, 1990, 101.
47 SCUDÉRY, 1973, 10:1132.
48 LA FONTAINE, 1857, 506.
49 SCUDÉRY, 1973, 10:1136.
50 On the Orangerie at Versailles, see HAZLEHURST, 1980, 126, 310; and WALTON, 1986, 141.
51 BABELON, 1999, 89.
52 CORDEY, 1924, 194.
53 SCUDÉRY, 1973, 10:1130.
54 CORDEY, 1924, 192.
55 SCUDÉRY, 1973, 10:1091.
56 MOLLET, 1981.
57 See BERGER, 1974, 321, illustration; HAZLEHURST, 1980, 276, illustration; WEBER, 1985, 92.
58 See BERGER, 1974, 317–319, illustration.
59 See WOODBRIDGE, 1986, 151, illustration.
60 See WEBER, 1974.
61 CORDEY, 1924, 192.
62 SCUDÉRY, 1973, 10:1136.
63 Quoted from BARIDON, 1998, 749.
64 SCUDÉRY, 1973, 10:1137.
65 CORDEY, 1924, 192.
66 SCUDÉRY, 1973, 10:1114.
67 SCULLY, 1991, 239.
68 SCUDÉRY, 1973, 10:1138.
69 CHANTELOU, 2001, 53 (translation modified); CHANTELOU, 1985, 25–26.
70 CORDEY, 1924, 193.
71 Ibid., 194.
72 MORAND, 1997, 73.
73 Quoted from VOGÜÉ, 1996, 6.
74 PETITFILS, 1998, 523.
75 MURAT, 1990, 344.
76 DESSERT, 1997, 340.
77 Quoted from PETITFILS, 1998, 449.
78 LOMÉNIE, COMTE DE BRIENNE, 1828, 157.
79 PETITFILS, 1998, 525–26.
80 Louis XIV, 1992, 88.
81 FOUQUET, 1696, 5:324.
82 FUMAROLI, 1997, 17.

SOURCES AND BIBLIOGRAPHY

MANUSCRIPT SOURCES

ARCHIVES NATIONALES, PARIS:
 FONDS D'ORMESSON, 144 AP 68;
 144 AP 72 (papiers d'Olivier Lefèvre
 d'Ormesson), microfilm: 156 MI 18,
 fol. 79 recto–88 recto; 156 MI 27,
 fol. 38 verso–46 recto.

SELECTED BIBLIOGRAPHY

AURICOSTE, Isabelle. 1990. Restauration ou
 régénération des parcs? L'expérience de
 Chantilly. *Histoire de l'art*, no. 12,
 (December): 97–105.

BABELON, Jean-Pierre. 1999. *Chantilly*.
 Paris: Scala. Translated by Judith
 Hayward as *Chantilly*. Paris: Scala, 1999

BALTRUŠAITIS, Jurgis. 1984. *Anamorphoses;
 ou Thaumaturgus opticus*. Paris:
 Flammarion; originally published as
 Anamorphoses; ou Perspectives curieuses.
 Paris: O. Perrin, 1955. Translated by
 W. J. Strachan as *Anamorphic Art*.
 Cambridge, England: Chadwyck-
 Healey, 1977 .

BARIDON, Michel. 1998. *Les Jardins:
 Paysagistes, jardiniers, poètes*. Paris:
 R. Laffont.

BECHTER, Barbara. 1993a. *Der Garten von
 Vaux-le-Vicomte*. Egelsbach: Verlag
 Hänsel-Hohenhausen (microfiche,
 originally Ph.D. diss. Mainz 1991).

————. 1993b. Der Garten von Vaux-le-
 Vicomte: Geschichte und
 Restaurierung. *Die Gartenkunst* 1:
 67–90.

BERGER, Robert W. 1974. Garden cascades
 in Italy and France, 1565–1665. *Journal
 of the Society of Architectural Historians*
 33, no. 1 (March): 304–22.

BLUNT, Anthony. 1966. *The paintings of
 Nicolas Poussin: A critical catalogue*.
 London: Phaidon.

BONNAFFÉ, Edmond. 1882. *Le surintendant
 Foucquet*. Les amateurs de l'ancienne
 France. Paris and London: J. Rouam.

BOYCEAU DE LA BARAUDERIE, Jacques. 1638.
 *Traité du jardinage selon les raisons de la
 nature et de l'art*. Paris: M. Vanlochom.

BRATTIG, Patricia. 1998. *Das Schloss von
 Vaux-le-Vicomte*. Veröffentlichungen der
 Abteilung Architekturgeschichte des
 Kunsthistorischen Instituts der
 Universität zu Köln 63. Cologne:
 Abteilung Architekturgeschichte.

CAUMONT, Gisèle. 2000. Liancourt. In *La
 main du jardinier, l'œil du graveur: Le
 Nôtre et les jardins disparus de son temps:
 Gravures du musée de l'Île-de-France*.
 Exh. cat. Sceaux: Musée de l'Ile-de-
 France.

CHANTELOU, Paul Fréart de. 2001. *Journal
 de voyage du cavalier Bernin en France*.
 Edited by Milovan Stanić. Paris:
 Macula-Insulaire. Translated by
 Margery Corbett as *Diary of the
 Cavaliere Bernini's visit to France*. Edited
 by Anthony Blunt. Princeton:
 Princeton Univ. Press, 1985.

CHANTELOU, Roland Fréart de. 1663. *La
 perspective d'Euclide, traduite en françois
 sur le texte grec original de l'autheur, et
 démonstrée par Rol. Fréart de Chantelou,
 sieur de Chambray*. Le Mans: J. Ysambart.

CHARAGEAT, Marguerite. 1955. André Le
 Nôtre et l'optique de son temps: Le
 Grand Canal de Tanlay par Pierre Le
 Muet. *Bulletin de la Société de l'histoire de
 l'art français*: 66–78.

CHÉRUEL, Adolphe. 1862. *Mémoires sur la vie
 publique et privée de Fouquet*. Vol. 2. Paris:
 Charpentier.

CONAN, Michel. 1981. Epilogue in Mollet
 1981.

CORDEY, Jean. 1924. *Vaux-le-Vicomte*. Paris:
 A. Morancé.

CORPECHOT, Lucien. 1912. *Les jardins de
 l'intelligence*. Paris: Émile-Paul.

DESCARTES, René. 1974. *Traité de l'homme*.
 In Charles Adam und Paul Tannery,
 eds., *Œuvres de Descartes*. Vol. 11. Paris:
 J. Vrin, 1974. Translated by Thomas
 Steele Hall as *Treatise of Man*.
 Cambridge, Mass.: Harvard Univ. Press,
 1972, 66–68.

DESSERT, Daniel. 1997. *Fouquet*. Paris:
 Fayard; originally published Paris:
 Fayard, 1987.

DEZALLIER D'ARGENVILLE, Antoine-Joseph.
 1709. *La théorie et la pratique du
 jardinage*. Paris: J. Mariette. Translated
 by John James as *The theory and practice
 of gardening: Wherein is fully handled all
 that relates to fine gardens. . . .* London:
 G. James, 1712.

————. 1972. *Voyage pittoresque des
 environs de Paris*. Geneva: Minkoff;
 reprint of Paris: De Bure, 1762.

FOUQUET, Nicolas. 1696. *Défenses*. 2nd ed.
 16 Vols. Paris: Vve Cramoisy.

FOUQUIER, Marcel, and Achille Duchêne.
 1914. *Des divers styles de jardins*. Paris:
 E. Paul.

FRANGE, Claire, ed. 1998. *Le style Duchêne:
 Henri & Achille Duchêne, architectes
 paysagistes, 1841–1947*. With English
 translations by Simon Lowndes.
 Neuilly: Éditions du Labyrinthe.

FUMAROLI, Marc. 1997. Foreword, in
 Pérouse de Montclos 1997.

GARNIER, Bénédicte. 1990. La création d'un
 nouveau décor sculpté dans les jardins
 de Vaux-le-Vicomte à la fin du XIXe
 siècle. *Histoire de l'art*, no. 12
 (December): 69–79.

GARNIER-PELLE, Nicole. 2000. *André Le
 Nôtre (1613–1700) et les jardins de
 Chantilly*. Exh. cat. Paris: Somogy.

GUIFFREY, Jules. 1887. *Comptes des Bâtiments du roi sous le règne de Louis XIV*. Vol. 2. Paris: Imprimerie nationale.

HAZLEHURST, Franklin Hamilton. 1980. *Gardens of illusion: The genius of André Le Nostre*. Nashville, TN: Vanderbilt Univ. Press.

JESTAZ, Bertrand. 1991. Documents sur l'œuvre de Jules Hardouin-Mansart à Chantilly. *Bulletin monumental* 149:7–75.

KELLER-DORIAN, Georges. 1920. *Antoine Coysevox (1640–1720): Catalogue raisonné de son œuvre*. Vol. 2. Paris: The author.

KERSPERN, Sylvain. 1996. De Vaux-le-Vicomte à Versailles: Les termes de Poussin. In *Nicolas Poussin (1594–1665): Actes du colloque organisé au musée du Louvre par le Service culturel du 19 au 21 octobre 1994*. Vol. 1, 269–84. Paris: La documentation française.

LA FONTAINE, Jean de. 1857. *Œuvres complètes*. Edited by M. C. A. Walckenaër. Paris: Firmin Didot Frères.

LA MOUREYRE, Françoise de, and Henriette Dumuis. 1989. Nouveaux documents sur Thibault Poissant (1605–1668), sculpteur des Bâtiments du roi. *Archives de l'art français* 30:51–71.

LOMÉNIE, Louis-Henri, comte de Brienne. 1828. *Mémoires inédits*. Edited by F. Barrière. Vol. 2. Paris: Ponthieu et Cie.

LOUIS XIV. 1992. *Mémoires pour l'instruction du Dauphin*. Edited by Pierre Goubert. Paris: Imprimerie nationale.

LUCAS, Michel. 1988. *L'ancien site de Vaux-le-Vicomte: Villages, hameaux, fermes et moulins disparus*. Le-Mée-sur-Seine: Éditions Amatteis.

MARIAGE, Thierry. 1990. *L'univers de Le Nostre*. Brussels: P. Mardaga. Translated by Graham Larkin as *The World of André Le Nôtre*. Philadelphia: Univ. of Pennsylvania Press, 1999.

MOLLET. André. 1981. *Le jardin de plaisir*. Paris: Éditions du Moniteur, 1981; originally published Stockholm: H. Kayser, 1651.

MORAND, Paul. 1997. *Fouquet; ou, Le Soleil offusqué*. Paris: Gallimard; originally published Paris: Gallimard, 1961.

MOSSER, Monique. 2000. Jardins »fin de siècle« en France: Historicisme, symbolisme et modernité. *Revue de l'art* 129, no. 3:41–60.

MOTTEVILLE, Françoise Langlois de. 1723. *Mémoires, pour servir à l'histoire d'Anne d'Autriche, épouse de Louis XIII, Roi de France, par Madame de Motteville, une de ses Favorites*. Vol. 5. Amsterdam: F. Changuion.

MOULIN, Jacques. 1998. La réinvention des parterres de Vaux. In Frange 1998, 28–29.

MURAT, Inès. 1990. Colbert. In *Dictionnaire du Grand Siècle*, 343–46. Paris: Fayard.

NICERON, Jean-François. 1638. *La perspective curieuse; ou, Magie artificielle des effets merveilleux*. Paris: P. Billaine.

———. 1646. *Thaumaturgus opticus; seu, Admiranda optices per radium directum, catoptrices per radium reflectum*. Paris: F. Langlois.

PÉROUSE DE MONTCLOS, Jean-Marie. 1997. *Vaux-le-Vicomte*. Paris: Scala. Translated by Judith Hayward as *Vaux-le-Vicomte*. Paris: Scala, 1997.

PETITFILS, Jean-Christian. 1998. *Fouquet*. Paris: Perrin.

PFNOR, Rudolf. 1888. *Le château de Vaux-le-Vicomte, accompagné d'un texte historique et descriptif par Anatole France*. Paris: Lemercier.

PINCAS, Stéphane. 1996. *Versailles: Un jardin à la française*. Paris: Éditions de La Martinière, 1995. Translated by Fiona Cowell as *Versailles: The history of the gardens and their sculpture*. London: Thames & Hudson.

POULAIN, Yvan. 1994. Les estampes d'Israël Silvestre et le décor sculpté du jardin de Vaux-le-Vicomte au XVIIe siècle: Le cas de l'Hercule Farnèse. *Revue de la Bibliothèque nationale de France*, no. 4 (Winter): 16–24.

Relation des magnificences faites par Monsieur Fouquet à Vaux-le-Vicomte lorsque le roi y alla, le 17 août 1661, et de la somptuosité de ce lieu. In Cordey 1924, 191–94.

ROSTAING, Aurélia. 2000. André Le Nôtre et les jardins français du XVIIe siècle: Perspectives de recherche et »vues bornées.« *Revue de l'art* 129, no. 3:15–27.

———. 2001. *Les jardins de Le Nôtre en Île-de-France*. Paris: Monum, Éditions du patrimoine.

SAINT-SIMON, Louis de Rouvroy, duc de. *Mémoires*. Ed. Yves Coirault. Vol. 1 (1691–1701). Paris: Gallimard, 1983; vol. 5 (1714–1726). Paris: Gallimard, 1985.

SCUDÉRY, Madeleine de. 1973. *Clélie: Histoire romaine*. Geneva: Slatkine; reprint of Paris: A. Courbé, 1658–62.

SCULLY, Vincent. 1991. *Architecture: The natural and the manmade*. New York: St. Martin's Press.

VOGÜÉ, Patrice de. 1996. *Vaux-le-Vicomte*. Troyes: La Renaissance.

WEBER, Gerold. 1974. Ein Kaskadenprojekt für Versailles: Zur Frage J. H. Mansart—A. Le Nôtre. *Zeitschrift für Kunstgeschichte* 37:248–68.

———. 1985. *Brunnen und Wasserkünste in Frankreich im Zeitalter von Louis XIV: Mit einem typengeschichtlichen Überblick über die französischen Brunnen ab 1500*. Worms: Werner'sche Verlagsgesellschaft.

WEISS, Allen S. 1995. *Mirrors of infinity: The French formal garden and seventeenth-century metaphysics*. New York: Princeton Architectural Press.

WOODBRIDGE, Kenneth. 1986. *Princely gardens: The origins and development of the French formal style*. London: Thames and Hudson.

ILLUSTRATION CREDITS

Unless otherwise indicated below, all photographs are by the author.

Bayerische Staatsbibliothek, Munich: pp. 90–91; Bibliothèque
nationale, Paris: pp. 40, 43, 68, 83; Bildarchiv Foto Marburg: p. 168
(left); Georges Fessy: pp. 14–15; Gérard Halary / GAMMA: pp. 29,
41; René Heckmann, Munich: p. 112; Institut géographique
national, Paris: pp. 19, 32, 174 (right), 183 (left); Ministero per i
Beni Culturali e Ambientali, Rome, Istituto centrale per il catalogo
e la documentazione: p. 89; Museo Firenze com'era, Servizio
Musei Comunali, Florence: p. 92; Nationalmuseum, Stockholm:
p. 44; private collection: pp. 10, 172, 174 (left), 175 (below),
182 (right); Réunion des musées nationaux, Paris: pp. 38, 57, 154,
158 (Gérard Blot), pp. 56, 168 (right) (Bulloz), p. 76 (Hervé
Lewandowski), pp. 105, 159 (N.N.); Service photographique des
Archives et du Patrimoine de Seine-et-Marne: p. 25; The Walters
Art Museum, Baltimore: pp. 94–95.

Longitudinal section (pp. 184–85) of the garden
at Vaux le Vicomte: © GeoGrafik, Axel Bengsch, Tübingen,
www.geografik.net

The work on the garden at Vaux le Vicomte enjoyed from the
beginning the generous goodwill and expert advice of Comte
Patrice de Vogüé, Château de Vaux le Vicomte.

Crucial support for the project was provided by Monsieur le comte
André d'Ormesson, who generously granted permission to publish
excerpts from the Archives d'Ormesson. Madame Aurélia Rostaing
of the Archives nationales, Paris, kindly assisted us in obtaining that
permission.

The preparation of the texts for this book was supported by two
meticulous and inspiring editors who pursue their calling with a
passion: Madame Françoise Bayle from the Art Lys publishing
house and Ms. Claudia Rudeck, Munich. Both these assistants have
earned the author's sincere thanks. The author is no less indebted
to Mr. Steven Lindberg, Berlin, who translated the text into English
with great sensitivity.

As a supplement to this book, there is an interactive
CD-ROM (text in French):
ANDRÉ LE NÔTRE, LE JARDINIER MAGICIEN
L'AVENTURE DE VAUX-LE-VICOMTE

Edited by the Fachhochschule München / University of Applied
Sciences, Munich
Information in French and English at:
www.fhm.edu/LeNotre

AUTHOR
Michael Brix, Munich

PROJECT COORDINATION
Claudia Rudeck, Munich, and Dirk Allgaier, ARNOLDSCHE
Art Publishers, Stuttgart

EDITORIAL
Claudia Rudeck, Munich, and Françoise Bayle, Versailles

ASSISTANCE
Isabelle Sauvage, Paris

LAYOUT AND PRODUCTION
Klaus E. Göltz, Halle an der Saale, Germany

LITHOGRAPHY
Scan Color, Leipzig, Germany

PRINTING
Offsetdruckerei Karl Grammlich, Pliezhausen, Germany

This book was printed on 100% non-chlorine-bleached paper
and meets the TCF standards

First published in the United States of America in 2004
by Rizzoli International Publications, Inc.
300 Park Avenue South
New York, NY 10010
www.rizzoliusa.com

© 2004 ARNOLDSCHE Art Publishers Stuttgart and Michael Brix

Originally published in German as *Der barocke Garten: Magie und
Ursprung* in 2004 by ARNOLDSCHE Art Publishers
Liststraße 9
70180 Stuttgart
Germany (www.arnoldsche.com)

2004 2005 2006 2007 2008 / 10 9 8 7 6 5 4 3 2 1

Printed in Germany

ISBN 0-8478-2606-6

LIBRARY OF CONGRESS CATALOG CONTROL NUMBER
2004090905